About the Author

Joan Baughan's early years were lived in the shadow of the 1914–18 War when the family moved to the safety of the country, to her Grandmother's house and a strict upbringing with a succession of governesses until her first school at 8 years old. Her teenage years were lived through a time when well brought up girls were still presented at the Palace, and not to even *think* of a career. They were expected to fill their lives with tennis, horse-riding and ballroom dancing wearing wonderful ball gowns; being showered with invitations for parties; attending banquets given by the Lord Mayor of London; once even a private visit to Buckingham Palace where she was shown round all the State rooms while the Royal Family were at Sandringham. A keen rider, she once rode her horse to Elstree Studios where it appeared in a film. Visits to Europe were an essential part of a girl's education and Joan saw Hitler and his followers at a ceremony held for the anniversary of the Black Death.

Then she met Norman Beck, a handsome pilot, and they fell in love. He started to teach her to fly, and they made plans to marry in June 1939. Then came the outbreak of World War Two and everything changed, for ever . . .

The Author
1939

The Inimitable Joan

The War Years
(1939–1945)

To. Pat.

with my best wishes.

Joan Baughan

Joan Baughan

A Square One Publication

First published in 1996 by
Square One Publications
The Tudor House
16 Church Street
Upton upon Severn
Worcs WR8 0HT
England

British Library Cataloguing in Publication Data is available for
this book

ISBN 1899955 08 9

Typeset in Palatino by Avon Dataset, Bidford on Avon, B50 4JH
Printed in Great Britain by Antony Rowe Ltd

Dedication

This little book is dedicated to the late Air Vice Marshal Robert Stanley Aitkin and the late Wing Commander Vivian Varcoe, for opening another door, and for all their kindness and understanding during the War years; not forgetting the many other splendid young men, all of whom aimed to give those of us who survived a better world to live in.

And of course, to Norman, killed in action 100 days after our marriage.

Shot Down

Smith got the chop last night, I watched him go,
A fiery streak across the savage sky,
Burning and breaking up, a crimson glow,
A fearful, searing, bloody way to die.

He only joined our Flight three weeks ago,
A timid little chap, devoid of fun
And ill at ease deep down, quiet and slow,
No time to make a friend of anyone.

Last night a fighter jumped him, belching fire,
The Wimpy shuddered, then blew up and spun,
Smith spiralled earthward in his funeral pyre,
Another grieving mother's only son.

Group Cap J. R. (Benny) Goodman

Foreword
by Group Captain P. D. B. Stevens

There have been many, many books and articles written about World War II and a good proportion of these have been autobiographies. But there has never before been one quite like this; Joan has written entirely from the heart and, as she passionately insists, every word is part of a true account of what went on around her.

Joan and Bacchus, her second husband, live in South Devon and my wife and I got to know them nearly 20 years ago. Theirs is a romantic (in the original sense of the word) story. Bacchus was best man at her wedding to Norman Beck just before the war; both were pilots in a Handley-Page Hampden bomber squadron stationed in North England and both were shot down at the same time carrying out a daylight raid on Germany. Sadly, Norman was killed, but Bacchus was taken prisoner and spent the next 5½ years in POW camps. Although he and Joan remained on friendly terms, it was not until 1954 that they decided to get married.

As you will read, Joan did not join the Womens' Auxiliary Air Force – as it was known at the time – immediately at the outbreak of war, but once she did, 'things happened'; and it is this very personal account of what did indeed happen, especially in her own sphere of activity when she was in the thick of things at Bomber Command Headquarters, that you are about to read. From now on, this is all pure and inimitable Joan.

Acknowledgement is gratefully made to the Copyright office of the Public Records Office at Kew for permission to reproduce the following material:

6729: AIR 14/3741   J. No 20496
         – Cologne Raid 30/31 May 1942

4117: AIR 14/3743   J. No 20486
         – Dams Road 16/17 May 1943

6242: AIR 14/3643   J. No 20496
         – Peenemunde 17/18 August 1943

549570: AIR 14/3743   J. No 20496
         – Munster 18, 18/17 night November '44

01510: AIR 14/3745   J. No 20496
         – Nüremberg 30/31 March 1944
         – Dresden 13/14 February 1945

*Norman outside the Officers Quarters
at R.A.F. Hemswell*

*Norman Beck in his Hampden
1939*

CHAPTER ONE

My War Years

My war years began three months before war was declared. I was married on Saturday 10th June 1939, to Flying Officer Norman Croxon Beck, and my name changed from Joan Evelyn Robertson, to 'Judy' Evelyn Beck, the Christian name being a nickname.

At the time of our marriage, he was twenty-eight years of age in the previous April, and I became twenty-eight in the August after our wedding. We were very much in love, and believe it or not, he asked me to marry him before even kissing me, and I remained a virgin until we married.

Very soon after the war started, the RAF dropped leaflets over Germany, informing the nation that we were at war to fight the Nazis. This started the 'pantomime'.

The first of such raids was on the night of 3/4 September and seven 'attacks' were made in the first week of the war. Whitleys were used for this purpose, and the leaflets were dropped through the flare-chute and scattered by the slip stream. Several further raids of leaflet dropping were made during September. The first raid of leaflet dropping on Berlin was on 1/2 October.

Aircraft from Finningley, another station in 5 Group, came over to us at RAF station Hemswell, also in 5 Group, and dropped 'leaflets' – sheets of loo paper! That was too much for our chaps, so we at Hemswell retaliated by bombing Finningley with 'jerries' – in other words chamber pots, that's the polite word! The 5 Group of 144 squadron were equipped with Handley-Page Hampdens.

Soon after this 'raid', Finningley came over again, and were met by a barrage of 'balloons' – in fact they were not really balloons, but inflated condoms. You can imagine the release of tension this caused. Those early days were really horrid, but although many of us felt that war was looming, we tried to push the idea under the carpet.

The few days before war was actually declared were most amusing. There were no other wives of the junior officers stationed at Hemswell, but I managed to fit in with the chaps Norman had as friends.

I shall never forget one night, when three cars were driving in formation along Ermine Street, the old Roman road, as straight as it was possible to be built. I was petrified. We were on a night out to Lincoln, where we all used to pile into the 'Snake Pit', a very small room in the Saracen's Head. I used to have to sit on top of an upright piano, or on the window sill of a high window, as there was no other space. We all drank beer at four pence a half pint. None of us suffered any pain and all the drivers were quite fit to drive – well, more or less. The next thing was to collect fish and chips, then on down Ermine Street to a green patch beside the road where we all parked our cars. Sitting on the grass in the late evening to eat our fish and chips was real fun. One night, after one of these evenings, I needed to use a bush, and told the chaps that I was going to stretch my legs, and to stay where they were. Suddenly I gave an almighty screech, as I had made contact with a stinging nettle in a very tender spot of my anatomy. Norman called out to see if I was OK. I told him what had happened; there was hilarious laughter all round, and soon we all returned home. The next day, and the day after, various chaps visited me with posies of dock leaves. What a laugh it caused.

During late June or early July 1939, Norman, with others, flew to Paris to give an air display. They had a hilarious time, as one can easily imagine, swanning in the evening, dining and drinking, with the result that they were late on duty the following morning. The punishment was confinement to 'camp' (the hotel) that evening. Wing Commander James C. Cunningham, who was in charge of the officers, had to stay in the hotel also, to be sure that none of them escaped. Goodness knows how it was done, but at some time they date-stamped the receptionist's bottom! Then the day came for their return. They flew over the keeper's cottage which Norman and I rented, terribly low, so that I could see all the nuts and bolts on the aircraft. It was terrifying. The aircrafts were loaded with booze, so the Station Commander, Group Captain E. A. B. Rice, had to 'phone customs to say that his officers had each brought in some wine and other alcohol. The all clear was given by customs, and a party in the mess was on. There was so much champagne and other wines, that some of the chaps tried to throw empty bottles through the wooden structure of the officers' mess. A Squadron Leader Derbyshire came up to me and said, 'Are you standing on your two legs alright?' I replied that I was, and he said that he was not. He had a wooden leg, which I did not know about until he told me! Norman kept his eye on me, and eventually came over to me and asked what I was drinking. I said, 'I don't know, but it's delicious!' He smelt it, and declared, 'We are going back to the cottage.' It was Pernod, which on top of champagne was a bit much. So off we went.

Our cottage was very cosy. It was semi-attached to one of the keepers' cottages on the estate. We did a lot of cleaning and fixed it up. There were oil lamps for light and for cooking too. The water supply was somewhat temperamental and sometimes I had to fetch water from the pump by the manor house. I had to use my baby car, an Austin 7, because the water could be so heavy to carry and it was quite a distance. Talking of water, taking a bath was a mammoth job. The bath was in the kitchen and had a large lid to cover it to make a table top. There was a copper in the corner and to light it and heat the water took a very long time, so Norman bathed and showered in the Mess. And I? I used to hang a notice on the back door saying 'Come back in one hour, Judy taking a bath!' On two oil burners and on a primus stove, I heated up saucepans and kettles of water, which I poured into the largest enamel circular bowl, with two handles. That went onto the floor, near to the back door. Since I filled it as full as possible, I slopped water when I sat in it with my legs outside. The water used to flow under the back door, with its worn-away step. After washing everywhere inside the tub, I had to wash my legs separately. The result of all this was, I was clean, my kitchen floor was washed, and the little yard outside the back door was also spotless.

We had another problem – hordes of cockroaches. We put powder down every night, and Norman went downstairs first in the morning to sweep up the dead and dying. Later Norman went into Gainsborough and came back with some other cockroach powder guaranteed to really work. It did, and they all went next door! I had never said anything to my neighbours about the cockroaches, so when they asked me if I had them I was able to say no. I felt terrible about all this, but spiders and the like were the biggest horror as far as I was concerned.

I must admit that I really had a wonderful time before the third of September 1939, when war was declared. I became a widow on 29th September 1939, after one hundred days of marriage.

On Wednesday the twenty-seventh of September, Norman was at home all day. He wrote letters to his mother, paid his tailor's bills, and so on. Then he suggested that we went on the lake. We were, as I said, living in a keeper's cottage on a large estate. We were allowed to use the little boat and row about on the lake. During this trip, we went amongst the water lilies. Suddenly I felt truly frightened. I asked him to take me ashore, as I felt the lilies were pulling at me, to drag me down. He said to me, 'You must not be afraid of drowning, it's said to be a very kind way to die, and unstressful.' It was on the twenty-ninth, two days later, that he was drowned after being wounded.

Early that morning I heard the aircraft warming up. But Norman had told me he was duty officer for twenty-four hours, and would not be back until lunch time on the 29th. So I turned over and went back to sleep. The dream I had is still vivid in my mind today.

I saw lots of water, and Bacchus Baughan, who was a great friend of Norman's, and best man at our wedding, coming towards me. I asked him, in my dream, where Norman was, and he only said he did not know. But I do remember all that water.

The real story was this. Norman was the first to be shot down over Heligoland, and Bacchus was shot down over the sea. There were five Hampdens on this raid, and none returned. However the Germans reported that two officers had been saved and were now POWs.

Extract from BOMBER COMMAND – The Air Ministry Account of Bomber Command's Offensive against the Axis – September 1939–July 1941 (HMSO)

During the first weeks of the War it was rarely possible to act on the information obtained by air reconnaissance, for the ships of the enemy remained too close to their bases. They cruised about at night, returning in the morning and remaining in port every weekend.

It was therefore decided that Bomber Command should undertake reconnaissance in strength, using aircraft equipped with bombs and ready to attack. In pursuance of this policy, a squadron of Hampdens patrolling the

Heligoland Bight on 29th September, in two formations of six and five, found and attacked two enemy destroyers. Owing to what appears to have been an error in timing, the two formations became separated, and when the second reached the area the enemy had been roused to action. The five aircraft composing this formation were intercepted. None of them returned, and the Germans claim to have shot them all down with the loss of two of their own fighters. The other formation, attacking the destroyers from 300 feet, was met with heavy pom-pom fire, and a well-aimed shell went through the nose of the leading aircraft of the first flight. It struck the pilot on the elbow causing him involuntarily to pull back the stick and swoop sharply upwards. The other two aircraft close behind followed their leader. All the bombs fell into the sea wide of their mark . . .

The experience gained from this raid and that of 4th September appeared to show that a level attack on heavily-armed naval vessels from such a low height was likely to prove a costly undertaking. Moreover, the

```
penetrating  power  of  the  bombs
dropped  is  uncertain,  and  the  risk
that they may bounce off the decks or
turrets very real . . .
```
This is the incident which cost Norman Beck his life.

So for over six weeks I waited and waited, hoping Norman was one of the two saved. Then the telegram arrived, reporting his death. The shock temporarily partly paralysed me. The other officer besides Bacchus who was saved was Bob Coste, a Canadian.

Soon after this dreadful shock, the Germans sent Norman's silver cigarette case, and silver chain with identity discs back to me, through Group Captain Burgess at Air Ministry, who asked me if Norman had at any time given me the key to the code for writing to POWs. I had to say no, he had not done so. Under his instructions I did try to write to Bacchus, but to no avail. But all his letters to me were seen by Burgess in those early days.

After Norman was killed, it was not only heart-breaking, but my parents had not been in favour of my marriage to Norman in the first place. My wedding had enabled me to escape. A bride's thrill, of a white wedding, bridesmaids and so forth, was not on. I suppose this was my punishment. But this attitude of my parents did not gain them much. It gave me untold happiness to see my friends, who had gate-crashed the wedding. They all adored Norman, who had the most noble character. He was always thinking of others, and never hurt anyone with a stray remark. He was completely unselfish.

Before we married, I was invited up to Hemswell, and various senior officers' wives invited me to stay. Everyone was full of praise concerning Norman, and I do know, had he lived, he would have gone far. He was a wonderful person, thus making it very difficult for me to ever consider saying 'yes' to marriage on the many occasions that arose subsequently, especially during the war.

So to return home was not a great pleasure. But I did have my wonderful and understanding Granny, who lived at home.

Since my RAF widow's pension was only £90 per annum, added to which I did have a little money of my own, to live alone would have been impossible. Had I been able to find a bedsit or whatever, I still had to feed myself, plus I had no qualifications with which to find a job. It was all a horrid nightmare.

Soon after this, I decided I would try to sell our Austin 7 and mentioned the fact to our local garage. A short time later, I saw two senior RAF officers coming down the drive at my parents' home at Bushey Heath, with 'scrambled egg' on their peaked caps. I nervously went downstairs to learn the reason for their visit. It was to cast their eyes over my baby Austin. We went into our rather big garage, designed for three cars. I was, needless to say, slightly overcome, because my car was sitting beside my father's Silver Cloud Rolls Royce!

I told the officer who was interested that my car went like a bomb, at which he roared with laughter. But I omitted the fact that if I was the one in the passenger seat, and it was raining, I had to use an umbrella. The outcome was I sold it to the Air-Commodore Robert Stanley Aitkin. From there on we became great friends, and this helped me so much to overcome my sorrow.

Stanley used to invite me to the Officers' Mess, and out to dinner and so forth. His wife Ena was seldom in the area, as she was nervous of air raids. She was very sweet, and they would take me out with them when they went on the odd trip. One time I remember, we were going to Tangmere. Shortly before arriving there we passed through a village that had been bombed by a lone aircraft releasing its bombs, I suppose to get away from one of our fighters. There was a sea of feathers, like snow. I have never seen anything like it.

As I have said Ena was very nervous and I must say we were living in what could be a hotspot. In Bushey Heath there was Fighter Command H.Q. and likewise Ack Ack Command H.Q. As the crow files, about two miles away was Coastal Command H.Q., literally across the fields at Northwood. We were very fortunate, the only problem we had was the six foot long casing left behind after opening and emptying the cargo of incendiaries. But since I was not always at home, I did not go through what those that remained at home did. So Ena could not be blamed for wanting to live elsewhere.

One day Stanley rang to say he was taking me out to dinner, to the Spider's Web on the Watford bypass, renowned in those days for good food, and that he had invited some friends. We were awaiting their arrival, standing at the top of some stairs in the entrance hall, when Wing Commander and Mrs Dalton Morris arrived. Stanley went forward to greet them, and turning to me said, 'Let me introduce you to the mother of my baby,' meaning me! I giggled but at the same time the expression on Wing Commander Morris' face nearly killed me. I looked at Stanley whom I knew was really enjoying himself, and amused by what he had said, and came clean that he was referring to the 'Mouse' as it had been named by Stanley, and not as I had used to call it, my 'Baby' car. Not a very satisfactory way to begin an evening!

It was about this time that I knew I had to do something, having been trained only in household management, by my mother and beloved Granny, who was living with us at this time. I was really going in at the deep end as a non-swimmer, as far as civvy street was concerned.

Then my father, who had many years previously been to a phrenologist to have his 'bumps' read, suggested I went to see Stackpool O'Dell, somewhere in the City of London not far from the Bank of England. It was a real experience. One sat down facing a blank wooden partition, then two hands came through two hidden holes in the partition, and felt all over one's head. I never saw the owner of the hands, who called out numbers to someone, also unseen. These numbers were all marked against paragraphs relating to one's character. I still have this book.

The outcome of this visit was a list of pursuits that I should consider regarding a possible career. The list, which I also still have, was the following: Art, Science, Photography, Infra Red and Metallurgy. So since my father was a Metallurgist, it seemed to me that I should start there.

I started working in a laboratory, analysing metals. I cannot really say I enjoyed it much, being the only woman except for typists etc. I used to hate going down into the foundry, with all the red hot metals and the dross that was taken off, because it could spit. But all this led me to becoming the first woman in those days to go out into the world selling 'Pig' or pure aluminium, steel hardeners and Broo-zinc, which we discovered, could take the place of aluminium, which was required for building aircraft. So, as Broo-zing only contained forty per cent aluminium, it was possible to sell without a licence. To sell any metal containing more than forty per cent for industry a licence had to be obtained, which was very difficult.

The hat industry, in Nottingham and area, used aluminium 'hood heads'. These were heads to mould and shape hoods, to turn into hats. So they found Broo-zinc very useful. It was also needed for vacuum cleaners and so forth.

My time of selling did give rise to some very amusing incidents. For example I was up in the Midlands and visited a very large steel foundry. Brookside Metal Company, for whom I worked, allowed me to hire a car and driver, since factories of such size are not always situated in towns. I always wore grey-tailored suits, black accessories and my silver fox stole, and carried a briefcase.

When I arrived at this huge steel factory, I handed in my card at reception, giving my name and company, and was shown into a very odd type of office. Seated behind a bare, plain table were two men, smartly dressed. I immediately started my business chat, when one of the gentlemen said, 'Are you interviewing us, or are we doing that?' With that, and when all was explained, we all fell about laughing. There was much effort on their part to try to persuade me to join their organisation. They were apparently interviewing possible PAs, or top quality secretaries. Their reception was slightly at fault. Instead I came away with a large order for steel hardeners.

All this living alone in hotels, and coming home at weekends, became too much, and I felt the dreadful loss of Norman's death. The doctor suggested that I did something nearer to my home.

I was very sorry to give up so soon, especially as I was really making very good money, as well as seeing industry really going full blast, due to the war.

I suppose, doing this work with metal, I could see the shortages arising for want of brass, copper, aluminium and iron etc. So I got hold of an ex laundry lorry (not a van), which was a bit temperamental, but it got there, and which I parked in our drive. It didn't quite go with the house and garden!

Then I collected students, young men, girls and mothers, and started hawking like a rag and bone merchant. The chaps yelled for saucepans and just anything metal. Old garden rollers we tied onto the back of the lorry. All this, and the escapade, was great for helping me to maintain a proper outlook. We had many hilarious moments. One time one of the boys brought out a bucket from a house, and started singing in a strong loud voice, 'I've a hole in my bucket, dear Liza, dear Liza,' and someone else would add some more lines. The householders flocked to their gates and fences, cheering us on. Another time, one of the boys came rushing along the road with part of a brass bed. Pushing it along on its casters, going 'Honk, honk!' as loud as he could, he brought many householders out to laugh and cheer, and encourage us in our work. Then we had to go and unload, drop helpers en route, and return home. My overalls, headscarf etc all went in to soak, as

*Mary Turner and myself
exhausted*

Any old iron

*Joy Blackwell and myself
and the old laundry van/lorry*

did I too! My poor mother was so sure I would return with fleas, lice and bugs, but I never did. I smelt strongly of disinfectant.

There were days when we collected cardboard boxes, papers etc from shops in the high street. I was always the driver and boss. There were different dumps for paper etc, and 'any old iron' went elsewhere.

A lot of folk thought I was degrading myself when doing this work. When I heard that, I used to say, 'Oh, I'll be OK, I'll wash and dress up and upgrade myself.' I must say, I would have loved to have heard my mother's response to any stray remarks she may have heard. One day, a family in our Avenue was moving away from the area and my mother was chatting to this neighbour, who had her small precocious child with her, who kept interrupting mother while she was talking. My mother flounced into the room and told me about this child, saying, 'I had to come indoors, I wanted to kick that child in the navel.' I was rocking with laughter, because mother was so gentle with the young and animals, and a real lady.

I worked in the canteen at Fighter Command, with Lady Joan Sholto Douglas. Her husband was commanding F.C. at Bentley Priory. Air Marshall Sir Douglas Sholto Douglas took over from 'Stuffy' Dowding, as he was known to us all. Pam, his daughter, used to come to the dances we gave at our house. Daddy, when building 'The Tarn' (so-named because of the lake in the garden where we had a pair of swans and various ducks, which supplied us with eggs) had a specially sprung floor put into the drawing room, for dancing. He was, like me, a very keen dancer. Daddy sometimes employed a small dance band. At other times we used a gramophone. We had plenty of room for twenty-five couples to dance.

During this time I met so many people, some most interesting: Norman Hartnell, The Marquis John Carisbrooke, Jim Mollison (who married Amy Johnson), Walter Pretty, General Wavell, General Gort and Field Marshal Smuts. I was often invited to dine in mess at Ack Ack H.Q., when ladies were invited. The mess at Hartsbourne Manor, a delightful place, steeped in history. Our house was built in the grounds. The Mills brothers, whose father was Bertram Mills and owned the circus, were highly amusing. I went out to dinner very often with them and others, in London and locally.

Various people in our Avenue and nearby, let their homes to people in the Services stationed in the area. Like us, they billeted officers and their batmen. We had seven bedrooms and the batmen used the morning room as their room, which had its own door on to the terrace.

In one of these houses, there was Wing Commander Veriker ('Winkles') Davis, known as 'Little Boy Blue', and the Marquis of Carisbrooke. We had Eric Frost and of course other officers, including a Roman Catholic Padre, who gave himself Communion every morning. His wardrobe was rather full of empty bottles when he moved on! Returning one day, my mother said 'Little Boy Blue was on the phone just now, asking if "RAF Comforts" was at home.' She told him I would ring back, which I did. He asked, would I please go and massage Winkles' back. I said I would as long as he or John Carisbrooke were there to see fair play!

It was at this time that Stanley Aitkin really took me in hand. He was so kind, and helpful too. I used to go on various trips with Stanley when Ena moved away. He, like me, wanted company. We were very open, which was nice. He was many years older than me and we used to be invited jointly to parties. Whenever we went alone, if in London or somewhere, I was given his little case to carry, or if dining, I had it between my feet, under the table. One day, I felt very daring and asked what was inside the case, and he told me it was his loaded revolver; and it was too.

He was in charge of Signals and often told me many top secrets. I shall always remember one night, when we were having dinner and he said, 'At this very moment the Channel Isles are being invaded.' I think he was testing me. In fact many times during the war he must have been behind me, but as I moved away, I seldom saw him.

Then one day we went to London and he stopped outside Adastral House and said, 'Go on in and join up, and say you want to be in Int/Ops.'

(Intelligence and Operations) We had discussed this on previous occasions, but I cannot say the idea excited me very much. However I did sign on as a lowly airwoman WAAF.

As I have already commented, I was often at Fighter Command headquarters and met many of the officers, including three or four Polish Air Force officers who were much older than me – but I did mention them to my mother, who invited them to share Christmas 1940 in our home. That was a great success, and they truly enjoyed the atmosphere of an English Christmas, in our house with all the various traditions.

During the course of the day we heard from them some of what they were suffering, knowing nothing of what was happening to their loved ones – wives, and young daughters. The Russians were sex mad, and if no women were about it was said that they visited the cow sheds . . . There are many horrid and awful stories concerning the Russians during the war, and when I eventually ended up at Headquarters, Bomber Command, I had many reports to read of their ghastly attitude towards the female sex. I could never trust a Russian, even today.

CHAPTER TWO

I Become a WAAF

The day dawned and off I went with my cardboard box containing my gas mask. At the meeting place, I, with the other 'cattle', climbed into the back of a lorry, then a train, then another lorry, and finally we were at the Innsworth camp. I was ready to go to an abbatoir! It was all ghastly. I swore inwardly that Stanley could have done this to me, and swore even more when I heard that the factory which made our knives, forks and spoons had just been bombed. So I ate horrid runny stews (cat or horse?) with my hand mirror from my handbag and a metal nail file. Baked beans were a real problem. If you took the plate up to your mouth, the juice and beans would overflow down your chin, and God knows where else. All this for four pence a day (old money!)

Our two weeks of square bashing, and learning

when and how to salute, were a real eye-opener. Some of the girls had not had the benefit of my upbringing, nor perhaps the education. I did my best with them, and those sleeping near to me put themselves out to help me and cheer me up. I did not moan, but perhaps they saw a sadness in my face and eyes, which changed somewhat when one girl said she would 'burn' my shoes over the Nissen stove (this meant break them in, I discovered) and burnish my buttons.

The big day came when we would know where we were going to be posted. My big dread was going to Hemswell in Lincolnshire, where I had lived with Norman. But I was sent to Swinderby, which was in another part of Lincolnshire. On the journey I met a girl who was a Corporal, and who was also being posted to Swinderby. She said 'Now leave everything to me, and keep near to me.' We went straight to a Nissen hut, and she rushed off and bagged the beds in a corner, next to the Sergeant's room, which took up the rest of the end of the hut where our beds were. It felt almost private and it had another advantage, being next to the sick bay where Barbara and I used to sneak out as though going to the ablutions which we had already visited, nip into sick bay, heat up a kettle and then fill up our hot water bottles! It was arctic weather in late 1941, especially in Lincolnshire. My mother used to send me cakes and other goodies which I gave now and then to the sick bay girls in payment for the hot water, and also to the Sergeant.

My uniform looked different from those of the other girls. It was in exactly the same style as the ones the others were issued with, but a girl at Bentley Priory (Fighter Commander H.Q.) was the daughter of a friend of my father and when she heard I was joining up she gave me her Saville Row uniform, made of the same cloth as an officer's uniform, so it did look a little better. The Sergeant mentioned above asked me to let her have my uniform if I should ever be commissioned. At a later date I sent it to her.

There were thirty-eight beds in the hut and you would have to go miles to find a more mixed bunch. Soon after we arrived, we had to attend a FFI (Free From Infection) Parade. It was so degrading it doesn't seem possible. Firstly our heads were examined for lice or nits, then up with our skirts and down with our knickers to have our fannies inspected. You would be amazed at the number of the girls who had either scabies or nits – ugh! The next parade was vaccination. Everyone was told to bare an arm. I bared the top part of my leg. The Sergeant said, 'Come now, I want your arm.' I replied that I was a ballet dancer and they must do it on my leg, and that was that.

The baths and other facilities were quite ghastly by the end of the day. After camp inspection in the morning, however, everything was clean and wonderful. So sometimes, coming off duty in the morning, I would hang around waiting for the duty officer to do her stuff and then I would rush in to have my bath. Often I would go into Swinderby on my day off and go to a hotel for a gorgeous bath which cost one shilling (towels supplied). Those were the best shillings I ever spent! I became very friendly with the staff, and I felt like a queen. After my bath, I went on to the hairdressers, where they kindly used some evil-smelling stuff, before shampooing my hair, which was long and done up in a chignon. The evil-smelling stuff kept the nits at bay. After this, a nice lunch and a film. Real high living, or so it seemed.

Headquarters was about two miles from the Waafery by road. When fine we marched to work, singing various marching songs. At mid-day we had a bus, which was also used when it was raining, to take us back to the Waafery, and return us for after-lunch duties. I was very soon on odd hours for duty, including whole nights and some half days.

After my first trip home, I returned to camp in my 'home made car'. What a car! It was a cross between a bathchair and a pram. I had an Austin 7 radiator, cut in half to bring it down in height, in order to make it look more sporty. There was a bit of room behind the two front seats for a suitcase and several large bottles of water, which I used for topping up the wee radiator. When I first got it, it had no floor boards and you had to cross your legs to drive. You could have walked along the road had you wished, with the car all about you! My father, however, had some floor boards put down.

The hood was rather like a bath chair canopy. You could always hear me coming because it had a huge fish-tail exhaust.

Before I actually brought my car back, I went to a farm next door to the Waffery to ask if I could leave it there. In return, I would help on the farm in my free time. This was all agreed. It was bliss, I really worked hard, raking, hoeing and rolling, with two huge shire type horses. I also helped with the lambs, and when the pig was killed, made sausages. My part of the job was to clean the intestines with two knitting needles, so that they could be filled with sausage meat! I kept my working clothes at the farm. My car was used for taking all the gorgeous pork pies to the bakers, to be steam-cooked.

Now a story about my bathchair/pram car. I was driving back to Lincoln after a seventy-two hour leave, and picked up an airman thumbing a lift to Grantham, this side of Swinderby. Then suddenly the windscreen was sprayed with water from my burst radiator. Whilst waiting for it to cool, we were deciding how to mend it. Being miles from anywhere we were desperate. My passenger, a Corporal, asked if I had any soap (which was rationed). We duly plugged the crack with soap, filled up the radiator with my stock of water, and off we set. But before long, our windscreen was covered with soap suds. So we had to abandon the car, which was now very near an airforce camp. Here, we 'phoned our units, and

I think we got a train, and for me a bus after our train trip.

After this episode my father bought me a little Morris Tourer, a four seater. I sold the 'home made car' to a band leader. I often wondered on how many occasions he was late arriving or never arrived at all!

On days, or rather nights, when I was free, I went to the local pub, halfway between the H.Q. and Waffery. I would slip in the back way, put on an overall, to cover up well, and do the washing up for them, for which I got a gorgeous meal. Lots of the officers came in, so it was like playing hide and seek trying not to be seen. No one at the Waffery knew what I was doing. With such odd hours, it caused no problems. I never disclosed to anyone what I did, nor where I went.

One day the Station Commander, Group Captain Satterby, sent for me. He had known Norman, but it was really the first time we had spoken to each other. He asked me if all was going well, and if I was liking my work. Then he told me that he was putting me up for a commission. This great news was a big boost for me, but Satterby did say it would take a while before I had to attend the Selection Board. It was quite a time, too, but the day arrived for my interview before the board in London. I was given a little leave, which was nice. For me, it was an amusing occasion. I entered a huge room, saluted, clicked my heels together, and nearly knocked over the foot I was standing on – but luckily I did not fall. How I stopped myself from giggling I shall never know. I stood before the Board, who were all women. What a bunch they were too, all spinsters I should think, to judge from their looks. They told me to take a seat, which I did, and crossed my legs, hoping that they would see how relaxed I was! Their first question was, 'What did you do before joining up?' I replied that I was the first woman to sell 'Pig Aluminium' in this country and immediately crowned it with, 'And I was also a dustman.' The answer I got to that was 'Well, that will do.' There was one officer who looked human and carried a half smile, which I did not miss. I was in and out in no time.

Then I started wondering if I had failed, and this gave me a little time to think that I had been a little foolish. I soon adapted this to a 'don't care' attitude, which helped me through many difficult times.

The outcome was that I had got my commission, but was not called to attend the Officers' Training Course at Loughborough for about six months. It was not until much later that I thought of a possible reason, which you will discover as I continue my story of life as a WAAF. I never won my 'props' or became a Corporal, but strangely it never once worried me. I could never be demoted, as I was the lowest rank one could be! Although I never told anyone, especially the other girls, of my commission, they did find out somehow. But I kept saying that I was not an officer and would not be until I passed, if I could, at OTU.

The Intelligence part of my work was very interesting. Most days I used to copy all the 'call signs' for the chaps to use when they returned from operations. These were changed daily and were usually 'run off' in time for briefing. One night I was in the briefing room sewing on a uniform button containing a compass, and sewing currency of the country where the raid was to take place into the shoulder pad of the uniform. I also gave out Horlicks capsules for them to suck if they felt hungry on the way back. On another occasion I was working in the briefing room when Flight Lieutenant Abbot asked me many questions about my life and so fourth. I told him about myself, and Norman being killed, and that Bacchus was a POW in Stalag Luft 3. That night Abbot was shot down and captured, and the next morning he and Bacchus had a long chat! So Bacchus knew exactly where I was and what I was doing.

One night I was at the pub, in the kitchen, when one of those serving behind the bar told me that a lorry driver had come in to say he thought he had hit a black dog. He had searched for it, but couldn't find it. The next morning I was walking to work, and when I neared the pub I started to keep my eyes open, and found the dog. He must have been thrown a good way because he was nearly in a ditch, and he was dead. I knew at once who the dog belonged to, as he always walked with Gus Walker (whom I had met before the war) when he was going out on operations. I took the collar off the dog, and then quietly went about looking for Gus. I just gave him the collar, and said how sorry I was, so that he would know that something had happened to his dog, who may have followed him to the pub. I told him where his dog was and he left at once to fetch him in order to bury him on the station. Gus Walker became an Air Chief Marshal and an international rugby referee; he survived the war and died in 1984.

Once, after having spent my day off living as a human being in Swinderby, I forgot to report at the guard room when I returned. I was safely in bed, and cocked an eye to see one of the officers checking to see if I had returned. I pretended to be fast asleep! But I was put on a charge soon afterwards, for 'being disrespectful', and was detailed to prepare vegetables. I felt really uptight since I did not feel I should have been 'on the mat'. So I pulled all the outside leaves off as waste, leaving the hearts to be cooked. This took very little time so I sat down and had a fag. I seldom smoked, but sometimes it calmed me down. In came the Sergeant, looking at the greens and saying, 'What have you done?' 'Prepared the greens as ordered,' said I. 'You don't do it like that,' said the Sergeant. 'Oh,' I said, 'That is the only way I know since I don't do the vegetables at home.' So I was told to clear off.

At home, Eric Frost asked my mother when I

was due back on one of my seventy-two hour leaves, since he wanted to take me out to dinner at Bushey Hall, a really beautiful hotel, with wonderful food and dancing too. Also, he had a partner for me, which was a secret. So the day came, and I drove home, still with no idea as to who was going to partner me. I fortunately had some lovely clothes, so off I went with Eric. We sat in one of the drawing rooms. Everywhere was so beautifully furnished. I sat on a sofa and Eric in an armchair on my left. I saw Eric look up, but pretended I had seen nothing, only to behold a man who had vaulted the sofa and landed beside me. Who was it? Robert Montgomery was sitting beside me. It took my breath away, because I had seen his film where he did just this. I cannot remember what the film was called. I must say that my evening was more than enjoyable!

One night, there was a very big raid somewhere in the Ruhr. Our crews had to fly about six hundred miles to their target, through ack ack, night fighters, searchlights, the lot, and to return. On this particular night, the 5 Group Commander joined in the briefing; opposite the dais was the board giving aircraft type, pilot's name and aircraft's identification (a letter of the alphabet), and so on. You can imagine the tension that emanated from everyone. The 5 Group Commander was Air Vice Marshal John Slessor. I had once met him with Stanley, but naturally I pretended that I had never seen him, and no doubt

Satterby would 'fill in'. To get to my office I had to pass through, parallel to the dais, and I was in and out, en route to signals and so forth. Once while I was passing through, Satterby said, 'Mrs Beck, do you think you could make us some cocoa?' 'Certainly, Sir,' I replied, 'With bubbles on top or without?' They fell about laughing as everyone there did. Perhaps I was not acting as I should, being the lowest rank possible, but I felt we all needed a release of tension. We suffered terrible losses that night, and the chaps returning looked like old men. It was another of my jobs to give them hot cocoa before interrogation and going to the mess for a jolly good 'nosh up'. I was asked years after, what I had done to be mentioned in dispatches. My reply was, 'I made cocoa with bubbles on top'.

Often after a night like this, I would walk across the fields on the farm where I worked, instead of going all the way by road. On this lovely morning I was walking along deep in thought, thinking of all the wives, mothers and girl friends who would be hearing their tragic news, as I had once. And there coming towards me was the WAAF officer in charge of the Waffery and two other officers, out for a morning stroll. I saluted them and made my way to pass. They asked me what I was doing and at the same time ticked me off for walking along making a footpath for German airmen to follow and bomb the Waafery. I nearly exploded, and wanted to say, 'What about you three adding six

bloody extra feet!' All I did say was that I had been
on duty for fifteen hours, I was very tired, and I
was looking to see how my drilling was looking,
and if any more lambs had been born, in order to
report to the farmer. I turned and walked on,
longing to look back, but I did not. Can you
imagine a woman like that in charge of lots of
girls? A hen-brained woman getting two-and-a-
half rings on her arm?

Some of the girls said to me one day, 'We are
getting letters from home asking us to write, but
we *have* written!' There was a chorus of 'So have I'.
I told them there was little I could do. In
intelligence was a measly wimp of a man, who
was full of himself. I got chatting to him one day,
on security, and then he told me that he opened the
girls' letters to see if they were disclosing any
information. (I knew that the only information
they would disclose would be about the awful
food, and the heartless women in charge!) I said, 'I
suppose you open and reseal and post them on.'
He blindly said, 'Oh, sometimes, if I have the
time.' Much thought was required before I acted,
but the dice were with me. The Queen Bee called
me to her office and she went for me, saying that I
was the instigator of all the trouble on the camp. I
asked what trouble, and was told that I should
know. Since my work, sleep, work in the pub and
on the farm left me with little spare time, I was
mystified. She ranted on. I told her I was innocent
of all her claims and demanded a court of inquiry.

She fell back in her chair and said. 'You can't do that.' I said, 'Try me.' I went straight to the pub, phoned Daddy and told him the story. He told me to go straight back and say that my father is sending his solicitor along, which I did. She was white and shaking. All this happened just as I was going on leave. On my return, she and one other administration officer had been posted. I have no idea whether Daddy spoke to Stanley or not, and it was a big surprise on my return to find that they had gone. I think it probable that this woman had delayed my call to the Officers' Training Course and denied me my 'Props' and promotion to Corporal.

I was at Swinderby for Christmas 1941, my third after the start of the war. The thought of a 'knees up' in the mess was a long way from my mind, so I volunteered to take on the job of Duty Ops Officer, if they thought I was capable of doing so, although at that time I had heard I had passed my selection board. The Int/Ops Officers were so thrilled to be free at Christmas that Satterby agreed to my standing in for them all. Satterby came in and said the mess would be sending me a hot meal, and before leaving said, 'Right Mrs Beck, you are in charge of the station, and I leave everything to you, even to a broadcast.' So the Sergeant in Signals, and one girl on the switchboard and myself were 'on our own' in the Station H.Q. I was allowed to use the 'phone to ring home, through the kindness of the girl on the switchboard. I was sitting on my own up on the dais, working on a tapestry, when the Sergeant rushed in from signals, to say that I had to make a broadcast, instructions from 5 Group concerning that night's raid. I said I couldn't do that. He replied that I must, as the Station Commander had put me in charge. The Sergeant switched on the microphone to warm it up. I was slightly nervous, but put over the message from 5 Group, not disclosing too much information. Then suddenly the ops room was full of Officers, and Satterby said, 'That was an excellent broadcast, loud and clear, but don't start another broadcast saying you felt funny all over!' They all roared with laughter. I remembered saying that to the Sergeant while the microphone was warming up. I heard later that my broadcast, heard by Officers and other ranks, made the whole mess rock with laughter.

Early one evening I was in my hut getting ready for a WAAF dance. Several of the other ranks would be there, but not many. I was far from excited about the evening ahead. Then a girl came into the hut to say that the Flight Sergeant wanted me in the guard room. When I got there, there was a great friend of mine, with two or three of his chums, all young Army Officers. It was all grins, hugs and kisses. Peter Blackwell, with whom I was very friendly, had found out from my parents where I was stationed, and had called to take me out. (Peter was a *very* good looking chap and was the only son of the Crosse and Blackwell

Organisation.) The Flight Sergeant was most amused and when she heard Peter discussing taking me out it was too much for her; she suggested that the chaps joined in the dance, with refreshments. They were game, and all had a brilliant evening. The Flight Sergeant used to ask me if they might be calling again, she was all starry eyed! But I never saw Peter again.

Talking about parties, my parents suggested that if I ever felt like taking some pilots home with me in my car, when I had a seventy-two hour leave, to do so. So I did just that. The lads were younger than me, or about my age. Poor devils, they were truly strung up. The fun we had in my open Morris Tourer, which took the four of us! We simply rocked with laughter. We left at about noon on the Friday and arrived home in time for some drinks and a super meal (Mother must have said the right things to the butcher!) My parents really put themselves out to care and entertain. That night, I was pretty tired, but wanted to listen to Churchill's speech. So I decided I would undress, get into bed and hear it on my radio. I said they could do likewise and come into my room. Only one put his pyjamas on, and he sat on the double divan bed, at my feet. After the speech, they played 'God Save the King'. The other two stood up to attention, and the one on the bed just lolled there. This was too much for the others. They got hold of Jim's legs, held them up as if changing a baby's nappy, and slapped his bottom. But three men and a girl on a divan was too much. There was an almighty crunch, and down went the bed in the middle. The top and the bottom came up to make the beginnings of a sandwich. I have never laughed so much. Then, on inspecting the damage, Jim said, 'Where can I find a screwdriver?' I gave directions to the garage and told him how to get in, and by great luck he came upstairs with a huge screwdriver. My father, hearing all the noise and then the quiet, came out of his bedroom to ask if Jim wanted any help. He murmured to my father roughly what had happened. 'Well,' said my father, 'My bed is OK. I wish you goodnight.' When Jim came into the bedroom, with this massive screwdriver, it was too much for us. Jim said, in his light Australian way, 'Well, I've never screwed a Waaf's bed before.' By this time we were all completely helpless. I was out of my bed, which was on its side, and we were laughing so much that we didn't hear my father come in with a pile of books under his arm. He just said, 'I have been down to the library, and think that these books may solve the problem for tonight.' He went out saying, 'Goodnight all, sleep well.' The books were put in the middle of the broken side, and all was well for that night and the following one.

I have forgotten what we did the next day after breakfast, possibly it was a visit to our 'local', nearby. But in the early evening my father organised a splendid night out. He hired a big car, which he usually did, to save him driving in the blackout. Also the car would be there at whatever time the chauffeur was told. So, off we six went, Mummy and Daddy making up the six. We went first to a theatre, where we saw 'Oklahoma', and then on to the Mayfair Hotel for a gorgeous dinner, and a little dancing too. On the next day, Sunday, we set off after a lovely lunch, for Swinderby. The sadness behind this tremendous leave was that all three were shot down less than ten days later, on their next big operation to the Ruhr, which was a hornets' nest of trouble. My mother was very sad, but so happy that they had laughed and laughed. She also wrote to Jim's mother in Australia, and Mrs Timms sent us several pounds of dried fruit. When I was in Australia, in 1952, I met Mrs Timms, it was so nice for us both to meet.

One day I thought I would try to hitch-hike, at least as far as the railway station. On this occasion, however, I had just reached the main road from the lane to the Waffery, when a lorry loomed into sight. I did my thumb act, the lorry driver saw me, and he decided to give me a lift. He pulled up, in I got, and guess where he was going? To Watford, about two miles from my home! After a bus ride, I was home nice and early. The lorry driver was very nice. He said he was making only a short stop, somewhere en route, and if I'd like to disappear for a moment, not to worry because he would wait for me. I had no need to leave the lorry, but on his return he presented me with some biscuits (which were rationed). Before we parted he told me when he passed the lane where he had picked me up, usually a Friday. He told me the time too, so that he could give me a lift on another occasion. But after this my father gave me my Morris Tourer, so I went by car, usually giving someone else in uniform a lift, which was company on that long drive.

One of the girls at the Waafery, I do not know her name, or where she worked, but one day when I was washing some undies in the wash house, she started to sing. It was simply beautiful. She knew many of the light operas. I spoke to her about her singing and she told me that she was a gipsy, so had never had lessons. I told her that she should try to find someone who could help her and take her under their wing. She was a real find, but I was unable to help her in any way.

Soon after this, I was posted to 5 Group Headquarters at Grantham.

CHAPTER THREE

5 Group and After

Life at H.Q. 5 Group was very different from being on a station, as everyone was kindness itself. They knew that I was waiting to go to Loughborough for my Officers' Training Course. I had a lovely billet in a huge private house. There was a large bedroom, beautifully furnished, with a bathroom. My hosts and hostesses were all very friendly. There were many people living in this lovely house, and mostly they were related to one another. The gardens were beautiful too. My only chore was to keep my bedroom and bathroom clean. I was allowed to wear my civvy clothes when not on duty. One charming middle-aged man living there took me under his fatherly wing. He took me out to dinner, and round to meet his friends. Once it was to meet a surgeon in a hospital, who chatted to us while he had a rest in the middle of operating.

The WAAF Officers were all so friendly, and I spent hours with them, since I was given no real job except to observe the workings of a Group H.Q. Then news came that I was to go off to Loughborough. The WAAF Officers wanted to dine me out in their mess, but the Officer in charge said it might be rather awkward if it were discovered. I know we did something to celebrate, but it escapes my memory.

Loughborough at last! We had lectures and talks etc, but the training was laughable. All the recruits were treated as if they knew nothing, it was really pathetic.

I must admit that I nearly disgraced myself one day. I was drilling a squad of would-be new Officers, when the male Sergeant roared at me to give the order 'About Turn!' only just in time to stop the whole squad from going down a steep bank. After this close one a WAAF Sergeant (who was also on the OTU course) and I went down a little lane and she taught me more about drill, so that I was prepared the next time. The male Sergeants, who were giving us instructions, addressed us as 'Ma'am' from the first day.

Very soon after we arrived, tailors from large shops and uniform suppliers arrived, to take orders and measurements for our uniforms. I had an account with Harrods in those days. They supplied, very satisfactorily, all that was required, which amounted to quite a lot.

From Loughborough I was posted to Lichfield, where my eyes were opened. The Intelligence Officer, Squadron Leader Jimmy James, who took me under his wing, was as mystified as I was as to why I was sent there, as I was the only very new WAAF Officer. The station was vast and security was extremely tight. Jimmy and I often went out at night on our bikes, around the station, which was patrolled by Service Police and dogs.

At this station they made gliders, which were very flimsy-looking things, packed parachutes, and practised ejecting from aircraft on to piles of mattress-like cushions. The training for rear air gunners, which I tried, was very hard. You sat in a large bowl, resembling a gun turret, where you saw a film of an ME 110 or FW 200 which you had to shoot at and make a 'kill'. The German aircraft coming in to attack you would be swerving and weaving, and your pilot would take evasive action when he was informed by his rear gunner that there was a German fighter on his tail coming in to attack. It was all fascinating and there was so much to see. It was a very sensitive set-up altogether. Bacchus met Jimmy James in the POW camp some time later.

After a very eye-opening three weeks, I was posted to Driffield in Yorkshire. Again I was billeted in a private house, which was a really lovely old Mill House. The owner and my hostess, was Mrs Down, who was a little older than me, and a childless widow. We both got on very well together. She gave parties, with which I gave a helping hand, although she did have some help in the house, and outside also. She also asked me to invite the odd officer to the parties. At this time I met the Colonel of a gunner regiment stationed also in Driffield. The parties we went to were hilarious.

I met many of the officers attached to this Gunner Regiment. One I remember very vividly, was named Johnnie. One day we went to a party, and I remember that Johnnie and I made two comfortable seats out of a pile of camouflage netting in the back of the truck. This amused the Colonel when he saw us. It was all such fun. Johnnie was killed later during the war in France. Dear Johnnie, he was sadly missed.

One night I was duty officer in Operations and Intelligence when a call came through from Group, (we were one of the stations in 4 Group) saying that all aircraft returning from a raid were being rerouted to land at Driffield because of thick fog at their bases. I asked how many; squadrons there would be, and at once got busy. I rang the Station Commander, who was in bed, as I had been (but in a made-up bed near the telephones.) Next, I had to 'phone the kitchen staff to tell them to prepare to cook up a good breakfast for the very weary returning crews. I had to hand over the keys for additional rations. By this time the Station Commander had arrived, and he was very impressed and delighted that I had done all that I had done, and complemented me. Then he looked at me and said, 'My God, you look great in trousers!' I was wearing my uniform top, cravat and trousers. I laughed and said I had dragged it all on over my pyjamas. So I suppose I did appear to be business-like in an emergency. He then told me that he had his pyjamas on too. Soon those poor chaps arrived, for hot drinks and interrogation. I hated this part, I wanted to cuddle them (but I didn't!) as they looked dreadful, and you could see all the horror of war on their faces.

One day a signal arrived to say that Air Vice Marshal Aitkin would be landing late afternoon, and staying overnight. I saw this signal, naturally, but did not say a word to anyone that I knew him. Just before he was due to land, I stood near Flying Control, but out of sight. I saw the Station Commander and Adjutant go out to meet him, and as they approached Flying Control I came slowly out. Stanley was so pleased to see me and we were all walking to the car when he said to the Station Commander, 'Oh, I'm taking Mrs Beck flying tomorrow morning.' The Station Commander could say nothing, but WAAF or WAAF Officers were forbidden to fly. The next day I was so excited because it had been many months since I had seen or spoken to Stanley.

So, at nine in the morning I was there, and so was Stanley, beside his Percival Vega Gull. We got into this two seater aircraft, a chap swung the propeller, Stanley explained all the dials to me, and when all was OK for start off, up we went. This was the first time I had ever flown. Stanley said, 'See that cloud up there, I'm going into it, then I can kiss you and no-one will see us.' You have no idea what he made that aircraft do, one minute it was upside down, next doing loop the loop. I was clinging to him, which he thought was great, he was laughing and enjoying every moment. We eventually landed and off he went to the Orkneys. I don't remember ever seeing him again, but he did telephone me on the morning I was sailing to Australia in 1951. While chatting on the telephone, Stanley asked me why I was going to Australia. I immediately thought up a reason and told him, 'I'm going to Australia to do some shark fishing!' When I arrived on board the P & O Stratheard, amongst the telegrams and flowers in my cabin was a cable from Stanley saying, 'Don't worry about sharks in the sea, but do look out for the two legged sharks!'

When I returned to the Ops room I asked a Corporal for a hot cup of coffee. When she gave it to me she said, 'Oh Ma'am, did you see that aeroplane doing all sorts of things in the air?' My reply was that I did not see it, I was inside it! She nearly fell over with the shock.

It was rather fun being an officer as opposed to being an aircraftwoman with no props on my arm.

The mess were having a big party; it was getting near Christmas but there were not yet any decorations. Soon after I arrived, I did start putting posies of wild flowers on the tables in the male officers' mess. I was not asked to, but thought it was a nice thing to do. When this big mess party was coming up, the Station Commander, a Group Captain, (I do not remember his name) asked me to do the flowers. Money for flowers was available and someone would drive me to purchase any that I needed. First I gathered some gorgeous chestnut leaves that had turned in colour but not fallen, and I bought some golden coloured dahlias to go into two huge vases in the rather fine entrance hall. I must admit I was quite pleased with it all. Elsewhere, I got some lovely background greenery (a lot from Mrs Downs) and picked many wild flowers and trailing red berries. The cost was hardly anything. The local gunner regiment officers were invited, and we had a super time.

Not long after this, I was sitting on a Court of Inquiry, when a signal arrived for me to report at Headquarters Bomber Command, which was a posting. Normally if one is sitting on a Court of Inquiry, one cannot leave the court. But this signal being a demand, and having been passed to the Station Commander first, I was told to pack and leave. No one could give any reason for this move, but I was soon on my way.

Being posted as an ordinary airwoman on a station, then to a Group Head Quarters, commissioned, posted to a top secret station, working as an Officer on a busy station in Yorkshire – I had done quite a bit! I had learned a good deal. So naturally I was more than curious to know what my next job would entail.

One pleasant thing about going to High Wycombe which was the H.Q. of Bomber Command, was that I would be able to go home when I had some leave, since my home was in Bushey Heath, about one and a half hours by car.

CHAPTER FOUR

Headquarters Bomber Command

I fear that I am not sure about the exact date when I arrived at Headquarters Bomber Command. I do know that Air Chief Marshal Sir Arthur Harris arrived at H.Q.B.C. on 22nd April 1942, and I arrived just after this date, having been told that we had a new chief.

My first days were very exciting; I was taken all over the place by the officer from whom I was taking over. In the first days I could see that it was going to be a very boring job. It would mainly be writing up accounts from pilots' observations on raids. How wrong I was!

I think that before I go on, I should explain the set-up of the Intelligence section, to which I was posted. It was divided into three sections, I, II, and III.

Intelligence I had two officers. There was

Squadron Leader Fred Lugard, a man in his late forties, who was known to us as Uncle Fred. The other officer was Flight Lieutenant Anthony Ireland, who was an actor, and a very good one too! These two officers were responsible for preparation of our aircrew for the possibility of being taken prisoner, including briefing them on escape aids.

Intelligence II had three officers, Wing Commander Arthur Fawcett and Flight Lieutenant Rosco Railton, and for a very short time, Flying Officer Betty Sargent. They were concerned wit shipping, which entailed keeping the movements of enemy warships and submarines under scrutiny, and cooperating with our air sea rescue boats.

Intelligence III was the section in which I was to work. My boss was Wing Commander Vivian Varcoe. Then there was Squadron Leader Gordon Donne, and myself, Flying Officer Judy Beck. Our responsibility was enemy defences: German fighter aircraft, gun sites, balloons and search-lights. We also kept charts giving the statistics of bombs dropped, number of aircraft on each raid, and losses.

My other work had not been done by the officer from whom I took over. This involved keeping my own large map of N. W. Europe up to date, giving the disposition of the entire German Air Force, and the locations of the German night fighters. This was all done with coloured flags, giving the type of aircraft; ME 110, FW 200, JU 88 etc. I was required to place them in their correct position on the map in my room, and the map in the Ops room. All this information came to me or Vivian from Station X, which was Bletchley Park in S. E. England.

The Ops and Conference Room, Intelligence Section, Codes and Cipher, and clerks' and Teleprinters' room, were all underground, and the entire place was called 'The Hole'. It was just an opening under a huge mound of earth and layers of concrete, with a single door and a guard. Steps led down to the Intelligence Rooms, and the other sections, and down some further steps to the Operations Room. The photograph in this book shows it as it was at the beginning of the war. I gathered from my boss Vivian that Bomber Harris had better ideas, so I will try to explain this huge hall-like room as it was in my time.

The Operations Room was very long, an oblong shape of lofty proportions. It was air-conditioned, had a rubberized floor and was entered by a single door. There were underground passages which led from near the entrance to the Ops room, to the Commander-in-Chief's office and the guardroom, as well as the main building where various sections had their offices such as signals, armaments and so forth. On the main wall opposite the door were three blackboards, each being about thirty feet by ten feet. The Commander-in-Chief only had to glance at them

Joan Baughan

Nerve Centre
*Beneath this grassy mound, covered with bluebells in Spring,
protected by deep layers of concrete, lie the
Headquarters of Bomber Command*

*The mind that plans.
The C-in-C at his desk in the Operations Room
who preceeded Air Chief Marshall Arthur Harris*

50

The Inimitable Joan

Operations Room.
The Air Officer Commanding-in-Chief, with his staff, plans the
night's operations. Deep underground, the room is lofty, quiet
suffused by a soft light shining from half-concelaed reflectors.
Its walls are lined with huge maps, charts and blackboards

51

to see at once the exact strength of every Group, the whereabouts of the squadrons in it and the total number of aircraft available. Another board showed which Groups were attacking the targets selected on the previous night. These boards were kept up to date, using chalk, by the Ops Controllers and clerks. Above the boards was a large clock, with below it the date.

On your right as you entered the Ops room was a meterological map showing the state of the weather, which was changed every eight hours. Alongside this map was a moon chart, recording the periods of moonlight and darkness throughout the month. On the opposite wall to the weather map, to your left as you entered, was a large map of N. W. Europe, which I kept up to date with my little coloured flags; this showed where the Night Fighter Groups were located. I had a huge step ladder with a little platform and rest for my papers and flags. I needed a large ladder because the map I used was much larger than the one shown in the photograph. The first days I used it, I had to wear trousers, then one day, in my hurry, I forgot. I received a 'Whoopee' cheer from the Controllers, so that was that, no more trousers!

The Controllers' desks were along the left wall, facing the Order of Battle, of aircraft available, etc. They had telephones direct to Air Ministry, Groups and Stations. I had to visit the Controllers on most days, particularly when there was a raid taking place that night, to get the times of T.O.T.'s (Times

Over Target), times crossing our coast out, and on return. Squadron Leader Archie Clayton, one of the Controllers, was such a dear man. Both he and his wife visited us and stayed too, after the war. He also acted as my broker for a while. Another Controller was nicknamed Onions. He was also very nice but I did not know him so well as the other Controllers. Foster, who suffered from poor health, was also a Controller. His wife was an artist, known as Marion Foster; she became famous for her delightful Christmas and birthday cards. She produced pictures of young horses, with flowers in their manes, and perhaps a butterfly on their backs, and so forth. They were truly beautiful.

There was a Naval Staff Officer attached to Bomber Command. It was his duty to advise the Commander-in-Chief on all Naval matters and give the views of the Admiralty. Likewise there was an Army Officer to liaise with the Commander-in-Chief.

In the centre of the room were large tables mounted on pivots, so that they could be moved very easily from the horizontal to the perpendicular. On these tables were maps for use for night operations. These were also available for when the Commander-in-Chief selected the 'Target for Tonight' at his morning conference. My Senior Intelligence Officer, Air Commodore Peter Paynter and my boss Vivian were always in attendance at these morning conferences. During

Christmas 1943 I helped to look after the young children of the wives and officers at a Christmas party. I particularly remember looking after Wing Commander Jack Kynock and his wife's 'pigeon pair'. And what a wonderful pair they were. Both weighed together 15 lbs when they were born. Jack's wife was a sweet person – really lovely, and a blonde.

After I had been at Bomber Command for a while, I used to have a smallish map of the area of the target, which was slipped into a folder covered with a fine perspex, and using special cinagraph pencils the route was marked out, giving times and Time Over Target. Then, first thing in the morning before the conference, I would phone Station X to find out what German night fighters were operating, and those were shown on the map (usually in red) in the area where they were based.

Whilst at H.Q. Bomber Command I made two visits to Station X. It was incredibly interesting. This was where all the code and ciphering was done, listening in to German controls, and learning their codes, in order to understand the conversation. But more of that later.

Our office was quite large. There was a Flight Sergeant WAAF always on duty, night and day, who took all calls coming into Intelligence. At the same time there was a Flight Lieutenant Duty Officer, who would act for the whole section by putting the call through to the right person, or if it was during the night, take messages. We had four

Wg-Com Varcoe   *Flt. Lieut. Cockburn*
Intelligence Room
Here, reports come in constantly from the Group Headquarters.
Pieced together, they form the great mosaic of operations control.

to five Intelligence Duty Officers on continuous duty in our office. One was Squadron Leader George Salaman, whose German was almost better than a German native's. He was at one time at the University of Heidelberg. When Rudolf Hess landed in the North, George was sent to interrogate him. After this trip we nicknamed him 'Thumbscrew'. Another duty Officer was Richard Murdoch, who was always amusing and cheerful. He was called 'Stinker' and of course later became a famous radio and TV personality. Freddy Cockburn was another, his was the Cockburn Port family. I do not have to say more about this. If the reader is Ex RAF he or she will know exactly the form! Cecil Langlands was a most attractive man, most agile and he always had many stories to tell, being Lord Derby's horse trainer. One could always be sure of an amusing Sunday if he was on duty. One day we had a cake in our office, along with a cup of tea. Although the cake was well wrapped up, it suffered somewhat when we used it for a short game of netball, with the air conditioning standing in for a net. This larking about did help us, because our work was very sad, especially if we had some bad losses. Frank Luke was yet another officer, but he was not with us for very long, being posted.

An amusing incident occurred one day. Thumbscrew and his wife Olive invited me to have some pre-dinner drinks in a Hungarian Restaurant in Lower Regent Street. We were not dining there, so were drinking in the 'Well' part of the winding staircase, where may others were doing the same. Suddenly Thumbscrew looked up and saw Stinker going up the staircase. So Thumbscrew yelled out, 'Stinker old chap!' Richard looked over the stair rail, shouting 'Thumbscrew!' and at once joined us. We four caused quite a stir, with people wondering who we were, larking about and laughing.

At Bomber Command my desk was near to the Duty Officer, but I had my back to him, and facing me, with our two desks together was the Squadron Leader, and behind him a map of N. W. Europe with all my flags, but not so large as the one in the Ops Room. My boss Vivian had his desk in line with the Squadron Leader, with his back to the map too. This arrangement was very good when we had something to discuss. In this office we also had a large board giving targets and times, number of aircraft on last operation, and the losses. This board was always saluted when we entered the office, first thing in the morning and again after lunch, when we were wearing our hats. It was done in respect for those missing or killed on the raids.

Off this office was the C.I.O.s (Chief Intelligence Officer's) office. When I first arrived at H. Q. Bomber Command the C.I.O. was Wing Commander Williams, and very soon after Air Commodore Peter Paynter took over. In his office was the safe containing all the Ultra Top Secret Files. The Duty Intelligence Officer on duty always kept this key. Sometimes, if I should want to use a file, I had to sign for it, even if it was only for a few moments. The C.I.O. also had another door, which led out onto a gallery type corridor, with a glass wall looking down into the Ops Room. Along this corridor were other offices.

The first office belonged to Uncle Fred and Anthony. The next one belonged to the American General of the VIII American Air Force (a bomber force).

The office after that was a spare Intelligence office, which was very private. But when I was working with my slide rule, while doing figures for my large statistics book, using this room was bliss, as there were no telephones and no distractions. One day, Vivian asked me to go along and chat to some chaps who were in this room, and who were really strung up, as they had to do a very tricky raid early next day. They were to bomb the doors of a prison somewhere in France, it might have been Amiens, to release two hundred hostages who were going to be shot. I can only remember the names of two of the officers and I believe that there were four altogether. One was Pat Sands, whom I often saw in the underground tea room, which only held about eight persons. Here we got a cup of tea and piece of cake, (made of sand?!) The other Officer was Jack Kynock. We laughed and managed to 'unwind' a little. I was very friendly with these two officers, who both visited us after the war.

Still in 'The Hole', was a long passage at right angles to our office, where Codes and Cipher Officers were on continuous watch. Then clerks from our offices, who made us coffee whenever we yelled for it, teleprinters' offices, then of course male and female loos for officers. So it was a very big hole.

Opposite the entrance into 'The Hole' was a very much smaller hole, which was where a certain amount of photographic interpretation went on. The main photographic work was centred at Medmenham in Buckinghamshire. The staff who worked in close co-operation with Photographic Intelligence at Bomber Command. The Commander-in-Chief liked to see photos of targets attacked as soon as they were produced.

The officer I took over from took me everywhere in the H.Q. to introduce me: Operational Research Section, Armaments, Signals, and even a visit to the two PA's to Bomber Harris, Peggy Wherry and Barbara Morton. The Commander-in-Chief, during his daily conference at nine a.m. to discuss the target for the night, would never have a woman in the Ops Room, so the WAAF Sergeant, who manned the switchboard, was replaced by a male during his conference.

The Officers' Mess was a very fine building with a large entrance, with steps and pillars. One day, I was on my bike returning to the office after lunch. The sun was shining and it was a lovely day. Many of the officers were sitting and lounging on the steps in the sunshine. I had to pass this lot, and as I knew most of them, I thought I'd give them an 'eyes left' and salute. I was a complete lunatic, as well as a menace on my bike! I parted company with my bike, by falling in front of everyone. My pride really took a fall, and it made everybody's day. I was unhurt and shaking with laughter, as was everyone else. I remounted and rode off.

The WAAF Officers' Mess was a short way from the RAF Officers' Mess. The married quarters became quarters in which WAAF Officers slept and lived, with one fairly large married quarter acting as their Officers' Mess, and huts built in the woods for airwomen. I am afraid that I didn't spend much time in the Officers' Mess. They were so curious about my work, especially after I had been there for a while, but I could not possibly say anything. When I was in the Mess for about half an hour before dinner, drinking my one scotch, having left my office well after six, I was ready for peace and quiet. After dinner, it was back to my room, the drawing room part of a married quarter, which I shared with another WAAF Officer. On occasions I then became another person, out of uniform, and into a housecoat and high-heeled shoes (to try to keep a decent shape to my legs), and I would either read, but only seldom, as I had a great deal of Intelligence matter to read up, or mostly I sewed and listened to my radio, or wrote letters. I was very tired sometimes, after a day in the office, and just lazed and slept. When I looked back to my first week, and also the extra work I had to do, it made me very content, because everything I did, had one aim, to win the war.

In my early days at H.Q.B.C., Squadron Officer Felicity Hanbury was also there for a very short time. She was very sweet, understanding and kind. We became quite friendly, maybe due to the fact that we were both young widows. She married again some time after the end of the war, as I did too. She became Dame Felicity Peake. She had a son a year before I had mine.

I think it was on one of my first days, in July 1942, that when the target for the night was announced, it was a raid on the 'U' boat pens at Brest, St Nazaire and Lorient. Our Intelligence was not very good concerning these 'U' boat pens, and our aircraft were unable to destroy them, but did plenty of damage around the area. We also suffered rather severe losses. The reason why our aircraft had no success was due to the fact that there was sixteen feet of concrete above the pens, which our bombs were unable to penetrate.

One of my extra jobs was to keep up my huge desk books, containing graphs and statistics pertaining to raids. They concerned numbers of aircraft on each mission, losses, bomb loads and so forth. I remember showing these books to the Duchess of Gloucester (now Alice, Duchess of Gloucester) who was truly very sweet. I was rather excited when selected to join in taking tea with the Duchess in the Mess. The room was not large and had only a few easy chairs. When she saw me, she invited me to sit on the settee with her. She is a sweet little lady, so natural, but a little nervous too. Another book which I had to keep up to date was known as the 'Blue Book'. It had to go to Chequers, not far away, for Churchill to see at weekends. On many occasions I took this book to Chequers. I remember one day Churchill's little Grandson, now Winston Churchill M.P., was standing on the steps and saluted me. On another occasion Churchill had not arrived, but was due the next day. The housekeeper asked me if I would like to look around downstairs. 'Oh, yes please,' was my reply. I saw Lady Churchill's little 'snug'. It was sweet and very personal, with lovely colours and covers, pictures and flowers. As one walked about, one could detect the strong smell of cigars which Churchill smoked. I was also told that often after a luncheon, Churchill would disappear into his snug for ten minutes' sleep, and on awaking was 'right on the ball'. In this book is a picture of the 'Blue Book' that I used to take to Chequers. The pictures came from the photographic section, who were in another hole nearby. The photograph shows Bomber Harris looking at the book.

As time passed, Vivian gave me even more responsible jobs. Gordon and I had to write up a report of all raids made, giving all details: number of aircraft, bomb loads, and types of aircraft. It also

'Bomber Harris'
Looking at the Blue Book which I used to take fairly often to chequers. On the left of Bomber Harris is Air Marshall Saundeley and to his left Squadron Leader Alan.

included the route to target with times, and the information given by pilots on their return, when they were interrogated by Int/Ops Officers at their bases. We had to try to give a picture of the raid, including sightings of aircraft being attacked by night fighters or flak, resulting in their being destroyed, probably destroyed, or damaged. All this information came to us on a teleprinted form, known as 'Z' form, from all Groups where aircraft were operating on any particular night. These 'Z' forms appeared very soon next day on our desks. Sometimes they were as long as sixteen feet. This became a pretty massive report, named Interception and Tactics Report, which both Gordon and I signed. I understand that these reports were kept in the War Room, but I have no idea where that is today. One time, Vivian asked me to do the whole Interception and Tactics Report, including my usual write up on sightings of aircraft. It was very exciting when Vivian really praised my work. Nevertheless, I was glad that it did not often happen that I had to do the work alone, and I still had all my other work to do.

Another raid that I shall always remember occurred on the thirtieth of May 1942, *see Interception & Tactics Report – App. A*. It was the first one thousand-bomber raid on Cologne. Those poor dear chaps had to fly about six hundred miles and our losses were bad.

We certainly had some pretty tense work to do, so it was always a great joy if we were having a

party to wish whoever was being posted bon
voyage and good luck from the Intelligence
Section. If it was a male officer who was leaving,
we had the party in a terribly small room, set aside
for any member of the Mess to be able to entertain
his wife or girl friend. These parties were lethal.
There were lots of assorted drinks and bits and
pieces to eat, always including little pickled onions
(which I could not stand). We would sing songs,
and someone would read out a valediction, always
amusing, to the chap moving on. Then, last of all,
the remaining drinks were put into a large silver
loving cup, from which we all had to drink.
Unknown to the others, I never took more than a
sip as one does at Holy Communion. The next day
the Intelligence staff looked green and grey. When
Betty Sargeant left, the party was in our Mess,
where we had the use of a room upstairs, which
was very nice, with good furniture and a chinese
style carpet, round, with a fringe, in the middle of
the room. We were two girls and six men. The radio
or gramophone was put to use, and we danced. I
was dancing on this central mat, with Vivian, who
said, 'It looks as though we are on a little island,
and the blue carpet is the sea.' The next thing, I
saw Uncle Fred go out and bring in the bucket of
sand, ready in case of fire, and he started to make
a beach around our island. Then Arthur Fawcett
said. 'I think there is a tropical storm brewing.' He
promptly drowned Vivian and me with soda
water! I cannot remember the outcome of all this,

but naturally Betty and I were not directly concerned with the more outlandish goings-on!

There were many 'light' moments between work. I have already mentioned Anthony Ireland, the actor. He used to come into our office to listen to the six o'clock news, and on some occasions, if he was a little early, he would sit on the corner of my desk and say, 'Judy, why don't you marry me?' I usually said that I was not in love with him. He would reply, 'You know you are made about me.' I would give him a little friendly pat and that would last for a while. Sometime later, I travelled from London to High Wycombe on the train with Anthony and was tempted to ask him why he had never married. He told me that there were very few wives who could stand seeing or knowing that their husband was making fond love and kissing an attractive woman on the stage night after night. I must admit that I had never thought of this. Anthony was extremely attractive, tall, dark and very dishy.

Anthony was not the only one who used to speak to me of marriage. One of the Intelligence Duty Officers, called Cecil Langland, was always asking me to marry him, if we were alone. He too, was again a very attractive man, and full of fun. He even pursued me after the war. He invited himself to 'The Tarn', where I lived with my parents at Bushey Heath. I was out and when I returned, I went to find my mother, and lo and behold, Cecil was there in the drawing room with her. Always beautifully attired, that day his outfit was completed with a rosebud in his lapel. He wanted me to wine and dine and to take me to a show in London. I remember going with him to see the Crazy Gang at the Victoria Theatre, opposite Victoria Station. We were in the centre front stall seats. Bud Flanagan came on stage, saw Cecil and said, 'Wow, Cecil, where did you find her?' After the show, we went back stage. It was hilarious. Another time, we went to the little cinema in Regent Street, to a morning perfor-mance, and when we came out I bumped into a friend, Jean Addiscott. I introduced Cecil, who at once said, 'Judy and I are lunching at the Belfry in Belgrave Square. Join us!' During lunch Cecil told Jean that he had proposed three times that morning. In the powder room after lunch, Jean said I was mad not to accept him, as she reckoned he was a catch. But there was one thing that made me decline. He promised me lovely exotic trips, clothes, jewels, everything, but no love.

I must admit that the Intelligence Section was not popular, because we did not mix socially with the other Mess members. We were all so happy, wrapped up in the work that had to be done, as well as putting our heart and soul into it too. We did not leave a single stone unturned, in case it caused death and sorrow.

The Ruhr Dams, Sorpe, Möhne and Eder, were attacked on the sixteenth and seventecnth of May 1943, *see Interception & Tactics Report – App. B.* Some weeks before this raid took place by 617 Squadron led by Wing Commander Guy Gibson (whom I knew in 1939, he was such a nice man), a very large model of the dams was constructed. I did all the enemy land defences, such as gun sites, search lights and balloons. I also checked tall landmarks surrounding the dams. 617 Squadron were using a new type of bomb known as Dr Barnes Wallis's Bouncing Bomb, which after being released on a low flying attack, would bounce several times before exploding, the intention being to attempt to breach the wall of the dam. It was a costly raid, in men and aircraft. Guy Gibson was given a V.C. and thirty-three other decorations went to members of the Squadron. There was a heavy loss of eight aircraft out of nineteen, with their crews of the RAF's very best men. Guy Gibson was killed at a later date.

In the late Spring of 1943, June Turner of Photographic Interpretation (in the small hole opposite our large one), came into my office to ask what aircraft it was that could be seen in a photo taken up on the Baltic coast. I told her there were no German aircraft in that area, and also that the object was small and odd looking, and suggested that it should be sent to A.D.I. (SC) Air Ministry. The outcome of this came about four to six weeks later, when the drawings of the V1 and 2 (the 'doodle-bug' and the big rocket) were on my desk, thanks to the efforts of one of our spies, who came up with the plans of the whole area of

Peenemünde on the Baltic sea. The rockets were
launched from pads at an angle to complete their
arc, as it were, to the U.K. Then came hundreds of
'ski sites' (launching pads for V1) along the coast
from the North to South West. Many times I gave
up leave and days off, and went back in the
evenings, in order to plot these site positions. Their
code names were names of birds. Incidentally,
almost five hundred V2 rockets fell on Britain in
February and March 1945. Bomber Command
attacked Peenemünde on the seventeenth and
eighteenth of August 1943 with five hundred and
ninety-seven heavy bombers, *see Interception &
Tactics Report – App. C.* Forty bombers and crews
were lost and thirty-two more were damaged. This
was not a very successful raid. Apart from about
seven hundred people being killed, they only got
a Dr Thiel, and another important scientist.

I have mentioned earlier that in my office I had
a map showing areas of the German Air Force. To
leave this for a moment, there have been times in
my life, usually whilst asleep, when I have had
very vivid dreams. Vivian took quite an interest in
these. One morning, I told Vivian that that night I
had had a very strange dream. In the dream, the
Germans were going to launch the V2 from aircraft
off our shores, and what is more, my dream was all
so vivid, so that I could see that the German pilots
were wearing yellow pullovers. Vivian roared
with laughter, and possibly made an apt remark.
Whilst drinking my mid-morning coffee, I glanced

up at my map, and I saw three yellow-flags, depicting J.U. 88's located in Holland. So I said to Vivian. 'There you are, those junkers are going to launch those rockets, stationed at Venlo, Eindhoven and Nijmegen.' Which they did start doing, but not for long.

Then there was the occasion of the Great Escape, when the Germans shot fifty of the RAF Officers as a lesson, I suppose, against escaping. I knew two of these officers, Roger Bushell and Mike Cacey. Quite out of the blue Group Captain Burgess, in Air Ministry, phoned me. When Norman had died he had contacted me, and I remembered him. He had phoned me to ask if I could go and see the girlfriend of Roger and the wife of Mike. Roger's girlfriend was Lady Georgianna Curzon, Earl Howe the car racer's daughter, who was living near Penn, and Marjorie Cacey was the widow of Mike. One of the officers working at Bomber Command offered to drive me to 'Meadow Sweet' where Georgie lived, and bring me back in the morning on time. It was most exhausting. Marjorie's alarm clock went off every hour for her to go through her beads, as she was a very staunch Roman Catholic. Those two poor girls suffered so much, but I found that it was much easier to get through to Georgie. In face we had a wonderful friendship and saw a great deal of each other, until I married in 1954 and we were posted to Germany. I must say that I really enjoyed visiting Georgie, which I did very often. She died in late 1985 or 1986.

There was a lot of curiosity about my work, which was Ultra Top Secret, and I found the senior WAAF Officers to be beyond the pale in their schemes to 'put me to the test'. There was one time when the Admin WAAF Officer in charge told me that I was to go to Windermere on an Admin course. I told her that I could not go. She asked me why not, and I told her that I could not relate, even to her, why not, and suggested that she spoke to my Chief Intelligence Officer. I have no idea what transpired, but nothing more was said about my going to the Lake District.

We had a Scrambler in our office, which I used daily to inform all the Group Commanders of any new enemy aircraft movements and gun emplacements, information given to me from London and Station X. The Sergeants always got everyone on to the 'phone at the same time. I would then speak to the various Groups and then go over to the Scrambler and doublecheck that all the Group Commanders were on the line, before saying what I had to say. Some months after my usual Group calls I received a letter addressed to: 'The Voice, H.Q.B.C., Blighty. Apparently it was from a Sergeant at one of the Groups, who used to hear my voice before broadcasting. Speaking of broadcasting, I often made broadcasts (under orders) to Northern France, which was somewhat alarming in a way. This, of course, was later on in the war.

In July 1943, after months of discussion between

Professor R. V. Jones (a really wonderful man and brilliant brain, in Operational Research) and Dr Dickens, who was at Bomber Command, it was agreed that they would start to use 'window', the code word for strips of tin foil about twenty-five centimetres long and one to two centimetres wide. This was dropped from aircraft away from the route of the bombers, and showed up on the enemy's radar. A few hundred such strips would reflect, on the German radar, as much energy as a Lancaster bomber. At about this time we heard the German reactions to our use of window, when dropped on a raid on Hamburg. A cow in the vicinity had eaten one of these strips and died. This made the Germans think that we were using chemicals. On examination they found the black paint used on the strips, (so that the strips would not reflect in the searchlights,) contained traces of arsenic!

Whilst on the subject of 'window', Vivian asked me if I would like to visit Station X and 'listen in' to the effect of 'window' being dropped. This was a fantastic experience. They made me so welcome at Station X, and showed me all the work they were doing. Then the hour arrived for action. Four or five of us sat in a small room and in one corner was a cubicle, looking like a telephone box. Inside this cubicle was one of the men dealing with the German Night Fighter Groups, who was tuned into the German radar stations in the vicinity and area where 'window' was being dropped, and listening to the Germans giving orders to the Fighter Groups to attack, not bombers, but strips of 'tin foil', since that gave the impression of bombers en route somewhere, whereas our bombers were really in another area. It was truly fascinating. All of this was recorded onto brass drums, the diameter being about two and a half to three inches. They looked like old pianola drums, of years ago.

On another occasion, it was much more exciting. The German Night Fighter Groups were required to rendezvous over Beacons given a letter of the alphabet for example Beacon 'D' or Beacon 'O'. On this particular night, the man in his cubicle was changing the commands given by a Group from the Beacon ordered, to another Beacon well away from our bomber route. Then you could hear there was real commotion taking place amongst the night fighters, until in the end we heard, 'It's a bloody Englishman' (in English.) All the German Commands were given in code, with which Station X was well acquainted. I had seen the list of coded phrases, but had very little time to learn it, except that when they had made a 'kill', in their glee, they said 'Sieg Heil'. The next night a woman took over the cubicle, so as to throw the Germans since they used a woman, but I was only there for one night.

On another occasion, while I was at Station X, our aircraft were laying mines, called 'gardening', in the area of Heligoland, where there was a lot of shipping. The pilots had to be terribly accurate in laying their mines, as the exact position had to be charted. Sometimes an aircraft may have had to make a couple or more runs. There was usually another raid elsewhere to distract German attention from our mine-laying in the North Sea.

One day a signal came through to the C.I.O. that Air Ministry wanted me to go to Delhi, to start up an Intelligence Office. Naturally I did not relish the idea, being happy where I was. The C.I.O. called me into his office, and told me about the signal, and hoped I would turn it down, as they were all delighted with my work, as well as my cheerful self, about the office. So, I stayed on where I was happy.

In 1943 the Colonel of the Gunner Regiment asked if I would have his beautiful Golden Retriever dog called 'Gunner', who was locked upon as the Regimental Mascot. This was great for me. I was allowed to have him at Bomber Command. It meant getting up very early, and I would go on my bike, with him running, through the woods. Very often I took him straight to the Codes and Cipher Officers, who had been on night duty, and they would take Gunner back to my room when they returned for breakfast and sleep. Sometimes they would bring him to my office just before I would be going off duty. So he had plenty of exercise, and added to this there was an officer who worked at the meterological board, who went

'Gunner' at H.Q.B.C.

Myself and 'Gunner' at H.Q.B.C.

74

for very long walks, twenty-five miles or more, and he asked me if he could borrow Gunner, which I was very happy about. Gunner obeyed every command, and was a real joy to have on a walk.

I was Orderly Officer one day, and had to take an inspection parade, which was in a clearing just off the main path through the woods to the main Bomber Command buildings and 'The Hole'. It was a terribly cold October morning and the three rows of WAAFs were blue with cold. They were not allowed to wear greatcoats until November. So I said, 'It's too cold to check your appearance, you all look fine, so I reckon we will do a few exercises to warm up.' I stood in front and did some arm swinging and jumping and so on. I dismissed the parade in a shorter time than if I had had to walk up and down the rows. I turned round to where Gunner was sitting to attention, to collect my gloves from his mouth, and there standing on the path was A.O.A. (Air Officer Administration), an Air Marshal. I went forward, saluted and said, 'Good morning Sir.' He said, 'Good morning, may I ask what you were doing?' 'Certainly. It is extremely cold this morning and those poor girls cannot wear greatcoats or gloves until the end of October. Thus, when they do arrive in their offices they are numb with cold, so I thought that instead of wasting time huddling around radiators to thaw out, some exercises to get the blood circulating was a good idea. After all, we must go into battle with a smile and work as hard as we can.' After this speech we had reached the H.Q. and his office. I saluted and went on my way, and there was no more talk about it. When I told Vivian, he roared with laughter.

One night, on one of the occasions when I was O.O., the guardroom rang to say that a WAAF who had deserted had been found. This WAAF had said that she would return to H.Q.B.C., but the WAAF Sergeant in the guardroom up north had asked me if I would send an escort guard to collect her. I remarked, 'You have told me that she has promised to return of her own accord.' I thought for a moment, putting myself in this girl's place, and thinking about how I would feel, if in spite of promising to return, they sent a horrid guard escort. So I promptly said, 'Since she has promised, I will accept her word to return.' Yes, you are right, that was another black mark for me.

The last occasion was when Vivian had managed to get from the American P.X. (a type of NAAFI) a large bottle of orange juice. It was magic when we were working every day underground, and in air conditioning, to have it during the evening, in my room. I kept the bottle in my wardrobe. The medical officer ordered that I should have sun-ray treatment three times a week for twenty minutes during my lunch hour. During the winter I never saw much daylight. He also suggested that I should drink fruit juice whenever I could. I noticed that the bottle was going down rather quickly, so I made a mark on its side, and sure enough, it was going down while I was not in my room. I had also missed some other things, nice fine stockings for one thing. Now to find out who was having my juice and other things. I took all the juice except for perhaps two drinks, and put it into another bottle which I locked up in the only drawer with a key. Then I 'laced' the bottle that I kept in my cupboard, with either Kruschen or Epsom salts, the one that hardly tastes. The next morning, no shoes or buttons had been cleaned, some doctored juice was missing, and the batwoman was in sickbay! I heard this from other complaining officers. I rushed into work and told Vivian, who said, 'Ring the camp police.' So I did. The result was that the police searched the hut where she slept, and found a suitcase full of serviettes, knives, forks, spoons and so on. This ruffled the fur and feathers of the Administration. I should have made my report to the Administration Officers not the Police. It was a bit naughty of me to do this, but I did what Vivian suggested I should do. Beside, I may have laced my orange juice for myself, and surely I could do what I liked with my own juice.

Then I was called to an interview in the Mess one lunch hour, to learn that a dead new-born baby had been found. Apparently it was born in one of the loos and flushed on its way. I was asked many questions, none of which I could answer. They asked about the girls that did my typing. I told them that I never looked them up and down when they came into the office. The Admin staff were so sure that I'd know something, but they were disappointed.

The American VIII (Bomber) air force were stationed in Wycombe Abbey. High Wycombe, which before being occupied by the Americans was known as Wycombe Abbey girls school of quite a high standard. I have no idea where the school went.

I came to know the American Air Force General commanding the VIII (Bomber) Air Force quite well, and was invited to many parties, getting a lift back in the morning with the General, who always attended the early morning conference in the Ops room. I slept with the American girls in one of the dormitories. The VIII Air Force were generally very successful in the daylight operations, though they often suffered heavy losses. They used flak computation to help provide cover to the Fortress bombers, the B17s. So it was arranged that I should pay a visit to the Americans at Huntingdon, to learn flak computation. This again caused a stir with the Admin. They wanted to know where I was going. I told them to ask the C.I.Q.

When I arrived at Huntingdon they were so kind and attentive. The work . . . was tremendous. They had four men and one officer. I could see that for me to do it on my own was not on. I contacted Vivian, who came up at once. I shall always remember the three of us, Vivian, myself and the American Officer, Errol Flynn, walking backwards and forwards on a stretch of lawn in the sun. It was decided that I should stay and learn the wherefore, which I did. It was, as I have already said, a tremendous challenge for one person, and a female.

I duly returned to Bomber Command. The next day, at the conference, the target for the night had been selected, and it was Münster, *see Interception & Tactics Report – App. D*. The Commander-in-Chief turned to Vivian and said, 'Let's have the view of your Flak King as to the route to the target.' Vivian said, 'I have a Flak Queen, not a Flak King!' The next thing, Vivian came up and said, 'Judy, do a flak computation on Münster?' Gordon was detailed to help me. Then I got on to the Met people in London, to get the wind velocity in the target area which was applied to our flak computations, and finally we calculated the best approach to the Target. This took about one hour and a little more. Vivian went down to the Commander-in-Chief to advise him of some massed gun sites but after he was informed about the wind, he agreed to accept the route that Gordon and I had worked out. The result of this raid on Münster was that we suffered no losses. The raid in Münster was 13th November 1944. None missing. A second raid was carried out that night and only 1 aircraft went missing. B.C. was going to start some daylight bombing, hence my visit to the Americans, who had had much experience with flak computation.

I came back from leave one time to find a note

in my 'in' tray, to go and visit the Camp Commandant. I did this by going down the 'Hole' and hatless. I went into his office, and said, 'I understand that you wanted to see me.' He then went to his safe, and brought out a paper for me to read and sign. I duly read this and it turned out to be an adverse report, saying things that were quite untrue. As I was reading this paper my blood pressure rose and rose. Then I turned to the Camp Commandant and told him that there was no way that I was going to sign something that was not true. He then told me that I had to sign it. I pushed the document over to him and said, 'Would you sign something that contained things about yourself that were completely false? If you would, I won't.' And I stormed from his room.

I rushed back to the office and told Vivian of some of the things I was being accused of, and that, as much of it was untrue, I had refused to sign. I have been told since that I should have signed it, but this girl refused. Vivian told me to go back and get the report. I went back to the Camp Commandant's office and asked to be allowed to take this accusing document back to my office, but my request was refused. So I asked for pen and paper. I was not allowed to copy it, but I put down some of the allegations that were made against me. It was reported:

1) I was very unsociable and seldom in the Mess. That may have been slightly true, but after a long and very busy day I needed rest and besides

there were forty or more WAAF Officers and not more than ten or twelve places to sit, and I was not a senior officer.

2) That I lived too near to my home. That was again rubbish. To reach my home, because I could not get petrol for my car, unless on duty, I relied on Vivian to drive me across country, where I caught two buses and the trip would take me nearly two and a half hours because of the need to change buses, and the long waits for the bus.

3) That I was not very good at my job. How could they judge, since I never once disclosed what I did?

There were about six accounts given about me, not one of them true. Since it was over fifty years ago, I am afraid that items that were far from the truth have escaped my memory, but if I carry on, you will realise the whole situation.

While I was on my second visit to the Camp Commandant, when I was unable to bring my 'adverse report' away, Vivian, the C.I.O. and the Bomber Command lawyer, Squadron Leader Heseltine, were all awaiting my return. Flight Lieutenant Robby Roberts, with whom I worked, (he took over from Gordon Donne) was there too. He was formerly a journalist on a national newspaper. I gave them the list of everything I was accused of, which in a way was a nasty slant on everyone in my section of Intelligence III. The outcome of all this, however, was that Heseltine and my C.I.O., Air Commodore Paynter, wrote a reply to all the accusations pertaining to me, to the Queen Bee of all the WAAF. I was given a few days leave after this, not that I needed it, but the C.I.O. thought that a few days off was a good idea.

On my return from leave, the Wing Officer in charge, plus a Squadron Officer (who I discovered was a lesbian) were not there at H.Q.B.C. Why, I wonder, did I always seem to come up against women who were jealous, I suppose, and could never be nice to anyone. This episode, I might say, did not give me any sleepless nights, nor did it have any adverse effects on my work. Nor were those I worked with upset. They, like me, just carried on. Perhaps, having read of similar occurrences at Bomber Command, I think that my declining to speak about my work must have been a large prickly thorn for some folk, who felt, possibly, that being senior in rank, they were entitled to know everything. But having signed the secret pledge to disclose nothing, I said nothing.

At this time I was sharing my room with a very nice officer, a little older than me, and we got along together very well, unlike another I shared with for a short time, for she used to play Walzing Matilda on her piccolo, looking at me over her spectacles. But to get back to Pas, her real name being Pasely. One night I was pacing the room, and I could not sit still until Pas said, 'What is the matter Judy?' My reply was, 'There are masses of hands trying to clutch me. I just wish there would be a big thunder storm.' This only lasted about twenty to thirty-minutes, but I was terribly upset, but managed to keep it to myself. In the morning, soon after the Commander-in-Chief's conference had started, Vivian rushed in and asked me to contact Station X, to learn what German aircraft were operating in the Bay of Biscay. At once I said, 'Oh no, that must have been the convoy!' (Which it was; it had sustained tremendous losses.) he at once asked what I meant, and I told him about all the hands trying to clutch me. If only he were alive now, he understood me so well, and was always so sympathetic, as I have said. He was great to work with. He made a second marriage, and was wonderfully happy. He used to talk a great deal about his private life, and his life before his second marriage.

We were all aware of the approach of 'D' Day, but the date and other details were very hush-hush. In fact, we seldom spoke about it. A few days only before 'D' day, some Officers from the 51st (Highland) Division visited us at H.Q.B.C. and a big party was held in the male Officers' Mess. It was real fun, with eightsome reels and so on. Luckily I was well acquainted with most of the Scottish dances. As we know, the 51st Division suffered terrible losses at Caen, so very soon after that super party.

On the morning of 'D' day, I was out very early with Gunner, on my bike, and heard aircraft. I looked up, and saw aircraft towing gliders, just literally feet above the treetops. Then I really knew. I said a prayer for them all. I could imagine their feelings sitting there in the gliders. I have, all my life, had thoughts for others, and sometimes it can 'sap one dry'.

So many interesting things happened to me. I used to liaise at Coastal Command, and on one occasion the Duke of Kent was there to attend a luncheon. I too was invited. It was not long after this that he was killed in an air crash in the North of England. I also visited A.A. Command H.Q. to meet their armament officers, and to learn all about the possibility of bullets ricocheting off an aircraft, and the resulting damage. These visits, including those to Fighter Command, were organised by Vivian. Because they were duty journeys, I had the petrol to be able to drive home, since, as I have said, all three commands were within walking distance of my parents' home.

I had a week's leave at one time, and my parents took me to Tenby in Wales. I was sitting with them, and was watching an Air Sea Rescue boat in the harbour, and the various men who appeared to be working on it. So, I told my parents, I was going to have a look at this craft. I approached with a 'Good morning!' and told the officer where I worked, and that I was most interested in seeing one of the 'A.S.R.' boats, since I was acquainted with the 'Orange Forms'. That did it. 'Come on board,' they said. They did not have to ask me twice. It truly was most interesting, with all the facilities on board to look after those in trouble and distress.

The Officer said to me. 'As a matter of fact, we have been working on one of the engines, and are just going out on a test run, how about coming with us?' It took me very little time to decide about that offer, so off we went. It was amazing how that craft travelled, it seemed to skim over the crests of the waves. It appeared to travel with no going up and down at all, even though there was a good sea at the time. I was allowed to take the wheel, and one really had to hold that wheel, especially at speed. It was not raining but the wipers were full on. So that little adventure was a real treat.

One morning the target Nuremberg was selected. I was rather sad about this raid. It was such a lovely town, full of history. I came to know my Germany pretty well. The first time I went there was in February 1934. That time I travelled with a German girl, landing at Wilhelmshaven. Staying with business acquaintances, then on to Berlin and Czechoslovakia, and this visit lasted about three months. I visited Germany in 1935, 1936 and 1937, and in 1937 was in Nuremberg when Hitler was about to hold his big rally. It was frightening. I was staying in Dresden and that night the troops marched to Nuremberg and rested during the day. It was really terrifying. The Germans were practising air raid alarms and you were not allowed to stay in the street.

Back, however, to the raid. Nuremberg was attacked on the thirtieth and thirty-first of March 1944, *see Interception & Tactics Report – App. E.* I shall never forget entering the office after that raid. I went limp and cold when I saw that ninety-six bombers were missing. My heart always went out to wives, mothers and girl friends, having been through it myself, my feelings were especially strong, I think. Then, some time after this, Dresden was chosen. Bomber Harris did not want to bomb this city, but he was ordered to do so, so on the thirtieth of February 1945 it was bombed, creating a huge firestorm, since nearly all of the old buildings were wooden. Then, this bombing was followed by another attacked by the Americans on the fourteenth and fifteenth of February, *see Interception & Tactics Report – App. F.*

It was soon after this that I received a 'bombshell'. My mother suffered a stroke, and it was impossible to get any help for her. My father asked me to go home, in order to nurse her. I was sad for my mother naturally, but to leave B.C. was almost as bad. All who knew me could not have done more for me. I was posted to Transport Command at Hendon, so it was not far to travel each day by bus and tube, but I had to settle things at home, using my bike to shop at nearby shops and rush off to work, to be there by ten-thirty. They were all, from highest to lowest, so terribly kind, shutting their eyes if I was late arriving, or early leaving. My work there was nothing really. I interrogated crews coming in from trips abroad and so forth. The crews must have heard whispers about me, and would load me up with goodies such as oranges, dates and other fruits. Then my mother had her second stroke, I was allowed to leave the WAAF. This was about a month, if that, before the end of the war in Europe, and it brought me a new life.

As I have said, I had left the WAAF but on V.E. Day Daddy and I went to Piccadilly Circus. I took no handbag and wore oldish clothes. It was quite fantastic, and brought a big lump up into my throat. We walked to Buckingham Palace, shouted with the others, then returned home exhausted. I was asked to many parties at A.A. Command's Mess at Hartsbourne Manor as well as RAF Bentley Priory. I wonder if I really enjoyed it all?

V.E. Day to me is more remembering than celebrating, but then I do rejoice for those who can rejoice.

Epilogue

Life was not bad for me, but I felt terribly lonely. It was quite another life. I was not envious of other girls welcoming their loved ones home, but I missed out in a way that I cannot describe.

I went abroad, however, to Denmark first, being invited to stay with the Baroness Wadell-Neergaard at her castle, named Egholme, near Scibby, North-West Seeland. She was so sweet and kind to me. She was Lady in Waiting to the Dowager Queen. The Baroness told me many very interesting things about her life. She was crazy about animals and birds and had fourteen peacocks. She invited me twice in all, to visit her at Egholme for long visits, and I met many interesting people.

I also popped over to Paris on various occasions, to relations there. Then, in 1951, I worked my way around the world, for twenty-three months. In Australia I worked first in a home for old people. That saddened me very much, so I then did some modelling. It was mostly top coats etc, in temperatures in the nineties! From that, I went to a sheep station on the Great Divide. I was rustling up sheep to bring them back to the station for 'wigging' and 'crutching'. My first ever time going down and crossing a ravine on horseback was hair-raising, but when I gave the horse its head it was not so bad.

After this I started dressmaking, but after two weeks I gave up. I phoned Elizabeth Arden to make an appointment for a haircut and facial, prior to finding a job, got a wrong phone number, and ended up, after training, running a Beauty Salon in Adelaide for Elizabeth Arden. My next move was towards home, visiting Fiji, Honolulu, San Francisco, Los Angeles, Hollywood, Las Vegas, the Grand Canyon and so on. I took two weeks by Greyhound Bus, from Los Angeles to New York, where I stayed with friends for two weeks. I came home on the Coronation Monarch, what a flight that was.

On my return I started organising my own Beauty Salon and products, in Beauchamp Place in London, then Bacchus arrived on the scene and changed all that by marrying me in 1954. Three weeks before our marriage, Gunner died, aged about fourteen. I knew he could die at any time, as he had a bad heart problem. I had my first and only baby in 1956, at forty-five years of age. He has never looked back. He joined the Royal Marines Commandos on a short service Commission, was injured slightly in Northern Ireland, and is now helping to run an Exeter business. He is married to a lovely girl and they have an adorable and beautiful baby son.

Joan Baughan

In the beginning of the second part of the Great War the Germans found themselves running short of Saltpetre, a component part of gunpowder. This gave the oppor-tunity of showing the official advertisement which appeared in the newspapers of Berlin:

```
              NOTICE
          Z () () () ()
```

```
The women of Berlin are commanded to preserve
their chamber lye as it is very essential to
the Fatherland in the making of nitre, a
component part of gunpowder. Wagons with
tanks attached will be sent through the City
daily to collect and remove same.

                                     Signed
                          VON  HINDENBURG
                             Commanding
```

A German soldier in the trenches, upon seeing this, wrote the following:

> Von Hindenburg, Von Hindenburg, you are a funny creature,
> You have added to this war a new and novel feature.
> You'd have us while every man was born to be a fighter,
> The women, bless their loving hearts, must save their pee for nitre.
>
> Von Hindenburg, Von Hindenburg, where did you get the notion
> Of sending barrels round the Town to gather up the lotion?
> We thought that women's duty lay in keeping house and diddling,
> But now you've put the pretty dears to patriotic piddling.

Von Hindenburg, Von Hindenburg, pray to invent a neater
And somewhat less immodest way of getting your
saltpetre.
For Fauleins fair, with golden hair, with whom we all are
smitten
Must join the line and jerk their brine to kill the bloody
briton.

The English soldiers added the following, returned to the Germans . . .

Von Hindenburg, Von Hindenburg, we've heard in song
and story
How women's tears through all the years have saddened
fields of glory.
But ne'er before have women helped their brave in field of
slaughter
Till German women dried their tears and went to making
water.

No wonder Von, your boys are brave, who wouldn't be a
fighter
If every time he shot his gun he used his sweetheart's nitre?
And vice versa, what could make an Allied soldier sadder
Than dodging bullets fired from some pretty woman's
bladder.
We've sometimes heard a subtle smell still lingers in the
powder
And when the smoke grows thicker and the din of battle
louder
That there is found to this compound, one serious objection
No soldier boy can take a sniff without getting an erection.
Tis clear then why desertions are so common in your ranks
An arctic nature's needed to withstand Dame Nature's
pranks
A German cannot stand the strain, for once he's had a smell
He's got to have a piece or bust, THE FATHERLAND TO
HELL!

Just after the war at a Reunion
Group Captain Pat Sands, myself and
Wing Commander Vivian Varcoe

Interception/Tactic Reports
1942 – 1946

Appendix A

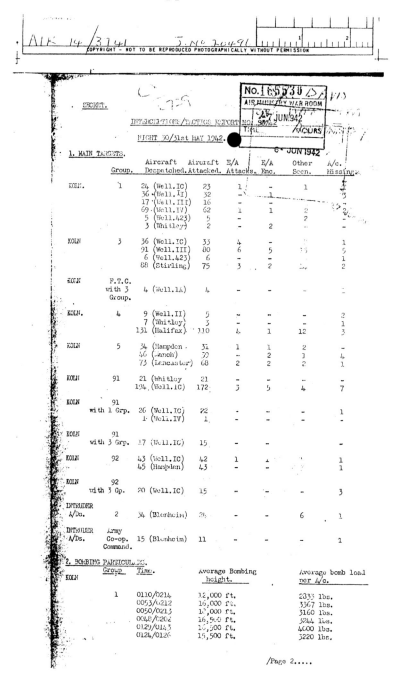

SECRET.

No. 65730

AIR MINISTRY WAR ROOM

17 JUN 1942

6 JUN 1942

INTERCEPTION/TACTICS REPORT NO.

NIGHT 30/31st MAY 1942.

1. MAIN TARGETS.

	Group.	Aircraft Despatched.	Aircraft Attacked.	E/A Attacks.	E/A Enc.	Other Seen.	A/c. Missing.
KOLN.	1	24 (Well.IC)	23	1	-	1	
		36 (Well.II)	32	-	1		3
		17 (Well.III)	16	-	-		
		69 (Well.IV)	62	1	1	2	2
		5 (Well.423)	5	-	-	2	-
		3 (Whitley)	2	-	2	-	-
KOLN	3	36 (Well.IC)	33	4	-		1
		91 (Well.III)	80	6	5	35	5
		6 (Well.423)	6	-	-		1
		88 (Stirling)	75	3	2		2
KOLN	F.T.C. with 3 Group.	4 (Well.1A)	4	-	-	-	-
KOLN.	4	9 (Well.II)	5	-	-	-	2
		7 (Whitley)	3	-	-	-	1
		131 (Halifax)	110	4	1	12	3
KOLN	5	34 (Hampden)	31	1	1	2	-
		46 (Manch')	39	-	2	1	4
		73 (Lancaster)	68	2	2	2	1
KOLN	91	21 (Whitley)	21	-	-	-	-
		194 (Well.IC)	172	3	5	4	7
KOLN	91 with 1 Grp.	26 (Well.IC)	22	-	-	-	1
		1 (Well.IV)	1	-	-	-	-
KOLN	91 with 3 Grp.	17 (Well.IC)	15	-	-	-	-
KOLN	92	43 (Well.IC)	42	1	1		1
		45 (Hampden)	43	-	-		1
KOLN	92 with 3 Gp.	20 (Well.IC)	15	-	-	-	3
INTRUDER A/Ds.	2	34 (Blenheim)	24	-	-	6	1
INTRUDER A/Ds.	Army Co-op. Command.	15 (Blenheim)	11	-	-	-	1

2. BOMBING PARTICULARS.

	Group	Time.	Average Bombing height.	Average bomb load per A/c.
KOLN	1	0110/0214	12,000 ft.	2833 lbs.
		0053/0212	16,000 ft.	3567 lbs.
		0050/0213	10,000 ft.	3160 lbs.
		0048/0202	16,500 ft.	3244 lbs.
		0129/0143	15,500 ft.	4600 lbs.
		0124/0126	15,500 ft.	3220 lbs.

/Page 2.....

ii

Appendix A

Page 2.

2. BOMBING PARTICULARS (contd:)

	Group	Time	Average Bombing height.	Average bomb load per A/c.
KOLN	3	0104/0220	13,000 ft.	2888 lbs.
		0045/0250	14,000 ft.	3347 lbs.
		0145/0155	15,500 ft.	4000 lbs.
		0037/0204	15,500 ft.	7714 lbs.
KOLN	P.T.C. with 3 Grp.	0130/0235	12,000 ft.	2495 lbs.
KOLN	4	0150/0210	13,000 ft.	3328 lbs.
		0202/0226	11,000 ft.	2300 lbs.
		0100/0240	13,500 ft.	734 lbs.
KOLN	5	0110/0158	11,000 ft.	1440 lbs.
		0110/0230	9,000 ft.	4377 lbs.
		0134/0510	14,000 ft.	6550 lbs.
KOLN	91	0045/0220	13,000 ft.	2640 lbs.
		0045/0220	13,000 ft.	1713 lbs.
KOLN	91 with 1 Grp.	0114/0235	14,000 ft.	2200 lbs.
		0135	17,000 ft.	1710 lbs.
KOLN	91 with 3 Grp.	0105/0206	13,000 ft.	2072 lbs.
KOLN	92	0050/0217	12,000 ft.	1556 lbs.
		0055/0217	11,000 ft.	1594 lbs.
KOLN	92 with 3 Grp.	0110/0217	13,000 ft.	3300 lbs.
INTRUDER A/D's	2	2355/0315	2500 ft.	1097 lbs.
INTRUDER. A/D's.	Army Co-op. Command.	0001/0119	3000 ft.	1092 lbs.

3. WEATHER.

    COLOGNE   Cloudless apart from varying amounts of cirrus.
                    Visibility good.

    ROUTE.   8/10 to 10/10 cloud over North Sea in layers generally
                    4/6000 ft and 8/10,000 ft, but cumulonimbus at times
                    extending from 4/15,000 ft with considerable static and
                    heavy clear ice in cloud.
                    Cloud breaking inland over Holland to nil.

4. ROUTES.

See attached Raid Track Map.

5. ATTACKS.

    1 GROUP.   (i) HASSELT 20 miles N.E. 0306 hrs. 16,000 ft. Wellington 102
                        attacked by ME.110 from starboard bow from 400 ft above.
                        ME circled port side of Wellington and fired a short burst
                        from port quarter which hit Wellington. Wellington
                        returned fire from rear turret and E/A broke away but
                        approached again from dead astern and fired another burst.
                        Wellington returned fire and scored hit on E/A which
                        caused E/A to lose height and fall away. Encounter then
                        broken off. Wellington hit in various places with cannon
                        shell and M/gun bullets.
                        No casualties in crew of Wellington.

/ii.........

Appendix A

ATTACKS.

1 GROUP (contd:)

(ii)   EUSKIRCHEN 0205 hrs. 17,000 ft. Well.IV attacked by believed
ME.109 which opened fire from starboard quarter and below
at 150 yards. Our A/C fire 3 bursts whilst taking evasive action
and it is unknown whether E/A was hit. E/A was then lost.

3 GROUP.

(i)   ROERMOND 20 miles W. of 0135 hrs. 11,000 ft. Wellington IC attacked
by unidentified E/A from port quarter. 2nd pilot killed. R/gunner
wounded, navigators hands burnt. No flak, S/Ls or I.F.F.

(ii)   TILBURG 0040 hrs. 16,000 ft. Stirling attacked by unidentified
T/E A/C. Evaded. No. S/Ls, flak, or I.F.F.

(iii)   DUREN 0200 hrs. 13,000 ft. Wellington IC attacked from astern
and below by unidentified SE/ A/C. R/gunner, navigator, WT/Ops.
wounded. No flak, S/Ls or I.F.F.
Return fire.

(iv)   COLOGNE 10 miles S.W. 0115 hrs. 12,000 ft. T/E. A/c approached
Wellington III from port bow. Opened fire which passed over our
A/c which dived to port. No I.F.F.

(v)   EINDHOVEN 8 miles W. of 0137 hrs. 16,000 ft. believed ME.110 attacked
Wellington III from astern and above. Firing short burst our A/c
evaded. Our A/c silhouetted by the moon. White ground lights and
occasional red lights seemed to indicate our track. No S/L. flak or
I.F.F.

(vi)   TILBURG S. of. 0154 hrs. 16,000 ft. 2 S/E A/c attacked Wellington III
firing short bursts from starboard quarter, beam and above. Our
A/c silhouetted against the moon took evasive action. No hits, No flak,
S/Ls or I.F.F.

(vii)   BLANKENBERGHE 8 miles E. of. 0239 hrs. 16,000ft. unidentified E/A
with S/L in nose which held our Wellington III opened fire with long
burst from port beam. Our A/c took evasive action. Was not hit.
No Flak, S/Ls or I.F.F.

(viii) OVERFLAKKEE. 20 miles S.W. of. 0050 hrs. 12,000 ft. Ju.88 approached
Wellington IC on port quarter then starboard astern to within 350 yards.
Our R/gunner fired two short bursts claiming strikes in nose of E/A.
which fell back into cloud with port wing dropped. Claimed as
possibly destroyed. No flak, S/Ls. or I.F.F.

(ix)   HASSELT 10 miles N.E. 0210 hrs. 14,000 ft. ME. 110 attacked
Wellington IC from astern on port quarter. Moon behind our A/c.
Crew wounded from one long burst, Wellington turned to
Starboard and F/gunner fired short burst in E/A which dived
away. No S/Ls, flak or I.F.F.

(x)   HALMSTEDE 15/20 miles 0230/50 hrs. 9000 ft. Wellington III saw Ju.88
2000 ft above 900 yards away. E/A shadowed for 15 minutes then attacked
3 times. 1st attack from above pulled up underneath and broke
to starboard. 2nd attack from starboard quarter to 200 yards broke
to port beam. 3rd attack dead astern and broke away below where it
was seen to fall away and burst into flames. Claimed as destroyed.
No flak, S/Ls or I.F.F.

(xi)   ANTWERP 20 miles N. of. 0015 hrs. 12,000 ft. ME. 110 twice
ineffectively attacked Stirling. No flak or I.F.F. but a S/L had
pointed our track crossing Dutch coast.

(xii) OVERFLAKKEE. 0012 hrs. 15,000 ft. M.E. 1000 passed ahead of
Wellington, fired one ineffective burst and disappeared.

(xiii) GLADBACH 0026 hrs. 16,000 ft. Stirling approached from below
by ME 110 with lights momentarily switched on. E/A approached and
was shot. Our A/c fired long burst starting fire in E/a starboard/
engine

Appendix A

Page 4.

ATTACKS.

3 GROUP. (xiii) engine and cock pit. E/A seen to crash and burn on ground and claimed as destroyed.

4 GROUP. (i) TILBURG area 0142 hrs. 15,000 ft. 3 E/A sighted. 1 ME.109, 1 ME.110 and 1 unidentified A/c. ME.109 approached Halifax to within 700 yards. on green quarter and opened up cannon fire without effect. No return of fire but evasive action taken. No. I.F.F. S/Ls or Dlck at the time.

(ii) HERTOGENBOSCH 0137 hrs. 13,000 ft. S/E. E/A. approached Halifax from astern to 300 yards and opened fire. R/Gunner gave one short and one long burst and saw tracer going into E/A which dived away and disappeared. A/gunner certain E/A was hit and its disappearance also bears to that conclusion. No I.F., No S/Ls - claimed as damaged.

(iii) COLOGNE 10 miles N.W. Halifax after encountering S/L and flak was attacked by S/E A/C from astern and slightly below. E/A tracer went high and R/gunner of Halifax gave one long burst at approx. 150 yds. range which caused E/A to stall while fuselage lighted up. E/A was seen to fall to ground and explode. No.I.F.F. E/A is claimed as destroyed.

(iv) AACHEN to N.E. 0215 hrs. 14,000 ft. After bombing the Town, proceeded on course of 209 degs. with full moon on port and clear visibility. There was no S/L, or flak, an E/A identified JU.88 approached below on port beam and openedfire at 300 yards, closing to 100 yards. Halifax dived and turned in to meet, as E/A climbed. Rear turret fired 1 sighting and one 7 secs. burst and mid turret one long burst. E/A went down and was seen to crash by all crew.
E/A fired with cannon and m/g and damage to Halifax consisted of r/turret damaged, all 3 landing wheels punctured, both oil systems damaged, petrol systems damaged, centre of port wing flap shot away. One Ju.88 is claimed as destroyed.

GROUP.

(i) ROERMOND 20 m. W. 0115 hrs. 10,000 ft. Hampden encountered S/E unidentified E/A. It approached Hampden from dead astern at same height and gave one short burst. Hampden dived to starboard and E/A overshot and disappeared. Hampden did not return fireand was not hit. I.F.F. not used.

(ii) COLOGNE 15 miles S.W. of. 0210 hrs. 14,000 ft. Lancaster sighted JU.88 crossing track 200 yards ahead and 100 ft. above. Ju.88 opened fire when dead ahead of Lancaster and its tracer was seen to go on starboard side of our A/C. Lancaster returned fire from mid-upper guns while making right hand diving turn and it is believed that the JU.88 was hit. It dived to port and disappeared. I.F.F. not used.

(iii) COLOGNE. 4 miles S. of. 0308 hrs. 15,000 ft. Lancaster attacked by unidentified E/A from astern. E/A fired short burst and broke away. I.F.F. not used.

91 GROUP.

(i) HOOK OF HOLLAND. 0200 hrs. 8,000 ft to 10,000 ft. Wellington IC attacked by 4 S/E A/C when passing over A/drome. No damage. No claim.

(ii) ANTWERP 12 miles N.E. 0230 hrs. 11,000 ft. Wellington IC attacked by JU.88 twice from starboard then port. No damage no claim.

(iii) EUSKIRCHEN 0110 hrs. 12,000 ft. Wellington IC attacked by ME. 109 Fs. No claim. No damage.

/ Page. 5.

V

Appendix A

Page 2.

ATTACKS.

92 Group.

(i) AACHEN 20 miles N.N.E. 0005 hrs. 13,500 miles M.E. 109 approached
Wellington IC (letter PI) from astern firing short bursts of
tracer. E/A then dived underneath and swung round to starboard
approaching to attack again from starboard beam. Our A/c took evasive
action turning towards E/A which was not seen again. No I.F.F.
No S/Ls.

6. ENCOUNTERS/OTHER A/C SEEN.

1 Group.

(i) ANTWERP 10 M. N.E. 0230 hrs. to 0246 hrs. 13,500 ft. Halifax
approached from port quarter same height as Wellington II. Broke away.
Halifax fired short burst which passed over Wellington. Halifax
disappeared then ME.110 seen which had been attacking Halifax.
ME then proceed to shadow Wellington from alternate quarters.
Wellington successful in evasion and after approximately 16
minutes E/A abandoned and not seen again. No S/Ls Flak or I.F.F.

(ii) MUCHEN GLADBACH 0139 hrs. 19,000 ft. believed ME.109 seen approaching
Wellington IV above and to port at 500 to 600 yards. E/A then
made as if to attack from green quarter but our A/c uncertain
whether bursts were fired. Diving turns made by our A/c which
did not fire and E/A evaded. No. S/Ls reported.

(iii) SCHELDT Estuary 0300 hrs. 12,000 ft. S/E E/A seen approaching
Whitley from red quarter and took up position astern. Our A/c
fired 3 short bursts at E/A 40 yards astern and closing. E/A not
seen again owing to evasion by our A/c. no. S/Ls or I.F.F.

(iv) COLOGNE 20 miles W. 0145 hrs. 14,000 ft. ME.109 approached Whitley
to 300 yards astern and our A/c fired 30 rounds. E/A broke off
evaded. No S/Ls or I.F.F.

2 Group.

(i) LOWESTOFT South of, 0233 hrs. 2,000 ft. unidentified A/c with headlights
seen astern of Blenheim and flying North.

(ii) VENLO 0004 hrs. 2,000 ft. one ME.110 sighted, and 2 other
unidentified A/c presumably on patrol.

(iii) VALENCIENNES 0030 hrs., 3,000 ft. a four-engined A/c seen landing
no navigation lights but exhaust flames seen. Flarepath on.

(iv) JUVINCOURT A/Drome 2350 hrs. 2,500 ft. E/A seen taking off. Later
seen to circle and land. Blenheim followed down and bombed from 400 ft.
at 2355 hrs. E/A believed destroyed.

(v) ST TROND 0115 hrs. 3,000 ft. E/A crossed behind Blenheim but did not
approach.

(vi) KNOCKE 2345 hrs. 4,000 ft. E/A with navigation lights sighted heading
S.W. E/A circled behind Blenheim but did not approach.

3 GROUP.

(i) COLOGNE 0110 hrs. 14,000 ft. Wellington approached at own level by
E/A with white light in nose. Both A/c weaved and E/A lost to
sight. No S/L.

(ii) OVERFLAKKEE 0205/0215 hrs. 10,000 ft. Wellington III followed by
S/E A/c for 10 minutes. Successfully evaded. No Flak S/Ls or I.F.F.

(iii) BRECHT 0200 hrs. 7,000 ft. Wellington III approached astern to
within 100 yards ME.109 evaded successfully.

/ (iv) .....

vi

Appendix A

Page 6.

ENCOUNTERS/OTHER GROUPS.

3 GROUP (contd:)

(iv) GILZE. 0019 hrs. 14,000 ft. possible JU.88 with white light in front and green in rear. Dowsed lights after turning into stern of Wellington III.

(v) BEVERLOO 0210 hrs. 11,000 ft. ME.109 approached from port. Passed at 600 yards to starboard quarter and closed to 400 yards. Wellington III evaded by violent action.

(vi) COLOGNE 20 miles W. 0145 hrs. 14,000 ft. S/E unidentified A/C possibly FW 190 (radial engine) passed 200 yards ahead of Stirling and turned into attack. Stirling dived, circled and evaded.

(vii) COLOGNE (121 hrs. 9,000 ft. T/E A/C, stub tail, fired red and approached from astern starboard. R/gunner fired 3 bursts. No.I.F.F.

(viii) ROERMDAEL 0210 hrs. 10,000 ft. ME.110 700 yards to port approached from moon, closed to 400 yards. R/Gunner of Wellington III fired 600 rounds E/A dived away. No I.F.F., Flak or S/Ls.

(ix) AACHEN 10 - 15 miles N.W. of. 0107 hrs., 11,000 ft. Stirling approached by ME.109. Our R/gunner fired short burst from 400 yards, and observed strikes on E/A before it disappeared. No claim. No flak or S/Ls, but red track-indicating flares had been shot up.No I.F.

4 GROUP.

(i) Position 51 deg. 23' N. 03 deg.00' E. 0317 hrs. 9000 ft. ME.109 approached Halifax on port beam and turned to get on tail of own A/c which took evasive action and dived into cloud at 7,000.ft and E/A not seen again.

5 GROUP.

(i) SCHOUWEN 5 miles. S. of., 0200 hrs. 10,000 ft. Manchester sighted JU.88 on starboard beam, E/A dropped below Manchester and then climbed to attack twice with Manchester in the moon. E/A remained at 600 to 800 yards same height on starboard quarter for 5 minutes following evasive turns by Manchester. Manchester increased speed, crabbed to starboard and E/A broke off. No exchange of fire. I.F.F.

(ii) Between OSTENDE AND ZEEBRUGGE 0317 hrs. 3,000 ft. Manchester saw 2 S/E fighters which were flying at very low level in same direction as own A/c. Manchester took evasive action and reduced height. No further incident. I.F.F. had not been used.

(iii) EUSKIRCHEN. 0215 hrs. 14,000 ft. Lancaster saw 2 HE. 113 approaching in line astern from red quarter slightly above. Sighed at 150 yards and closed to 100 yards. Lancaster did steep turn to port and lost E/A. No fire exchanged and I.F.F not used.

(iv) AACHEN 0150 hrs. 10,000 ft. unidentified E/A approached Hampden on starboard quarter showing bright yellow headlamp. First sighted 3000 ft. below. Successful evasive action taken. Whitley was then observed passed Hampden on port side and E/A appeared to pursue it. Both A/c lost to view. 10 minutes later two large yellow bursts seen ahead in the air giving the impression of two A/c bursting into flames and going down. Subsequently two fires seen on ground about two miles apart. I.F.F. not used.

(v) TURNHOUT 5 miles S. of 0243 hrs. 17,000 ft. S/E E/A approached Lancaster from port beam 1000 yards away at same height and closed to 800 yards. Lancaster took evasive action by diving to port and E/A lost to view. E/A carried light in nose. I.F.F. not used.

/Page 7......

vii

Appendix A

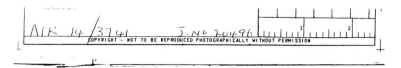

Page 7.

ENCOUNTERS AND OTHER A/C SEEN.

1 GROUP.

(i) ZWINDRECHT (20 miles S.S.W. Rotterdam) 0200 hrs. 7,000 ft. Believed JU.88 with single red light in nose travelling from dead astern in same direction as Wellington. Attacked by Wellington with 6 second burst. No result seen. No reply. No C/L or I.F.F.

(ii) ANTWERP 25 miles E.N.E. 0217 hrs. 12,000 ft. ME.110 prepared to make astern attack. Violent evasive action taken by Wellington 1C which shook off E/A. No rounds fired.

(iii) COLOGNE 20 miles S.W. 0150 hrs. 12,000 ft. ME.109 approached from astern to port side of Wellington 1C. E/A silhouetted against moon our R/gunner gave short burst and E/A disappeared.

(iv) MUNCHEN – GLADBACH S.W. of. 0120 hrs. 10,000 ft. ME. 110 crossed Wellington 1C heading S. same height. F/gunner gave two bursts. R/gunner one burst. No results seen.

(v) ACHEN 5 miles N. 10,000 ft. 0200 hrs. Wellington 1C followed dead astern by S/E A/c at 500 ft. below for 4 minutes. Evading action taken. E/A disappeared.

In addition to the above encounters, there were many sightings of E/A. which have been summarised as follows : –

AREA.	M.E.109.	S/E.	ME.110.	JU.88	T/E.	U/I
Coastal areas en route to Target.	1	2	2	3	1	–
S.Holland, en route to Target.	2.	4.	2.	1	–	1
Target area.	9 + 1 formation of 15.	15 + 1 formation of 5.	8	5	–	7
S.Holland. en route to Target.	2.	8	1	–	–	–
Coastal areas en route home.	4.	3	1	–	–	–

7. FLAK/SEARCHLIGHTS/OTHER AIDS TO DEFENCE.

COLOGNE. Heavy and light flak slight to moderate. Defences appeared confused as the raid developed and decreased in intensity. Searchlight activity was also less than usual and horizontal beams were employed to create dazzle and obscure the target.

Both flak and searchlights were generally inaccurate but individual aircraft were occasionally illuminated and heavily engaged.

Balloons were reported by many aircraft up to 10,000 ft. both in the centre and around the town.

ANTWERP. 3 – 4 balloons seen in the estuary N.W. of the town.

/Page 8 ....

Appendix A

Page 8.

8. WIRELESS INTELLIGENCE.

Identified night fighers units heard operating were :-

C057/0343	I/III/NJG.1	13 A/C. DEELEN, VENLO, TWENTE.
0105/0214	I/NGJ.5.	2 A/c. VECHTA.
C127/C512	II/III/NJG.2	4 A/c. GILZE RIJEN, LEEU ARDEN.

2.   It is estimated that approximately 36 sorties were flown by controlled night fighters. Identified areas of activity were CENTRAL HOLLAND, THE HAGUE/SOEST.RBERG, AACHEN/KOLN and possibly AMSTERDAM.

3.   22 attempted interceptions were heard and there were thirteen inconclusive combats, three in the HAGUE/SOESTERBENG area; five in the ACHEN/KOLN area; four in CENTRAL HOLLAND and one in an unlocated area.

4.   British aircraft were reported destroyed in the HAGUE/SOESTERBERG area at C053 and C212 hours, but at 0223 the control in this area reported seven British Aircraft destroyed in all. Further reports of British A/c destroyed were intercepted at : 0050 and C126 in the AACHEN area; at 0031, C157, 0207, 0220, C222 and 0343 in CENTRAL HOLLAND.

9.   OWN OBSERVATIONS.

1 GROUP.

i)   COLOGNE 15 miles W. of., C155 hrs. 17,000 ft. A/c in S/L cone hit by flak caught fire and crashed.

ii)   ROTTERDAM 20 miles S. 0116 hrs. 10,500 ft. A/c seen to fall in flames from own height.

2 GROUP.

i.   SCHOUWEN ISLAND 1037 Hrs. 200 ft. A/C seen to crash in sea in flames.

3 GROUP.

i)   COLOGNE 15 miles W. of. C215 hrs. 11,500 ft. A/c seen falling in flames after what was believed to be an attack by E/A. Tracer seen coming from below our A/c.

ii)   COLOGNE 3 miles N. 0140 hrs. 14,000 ft. A/C held in S/L cone and engaged by heavy flak seen losing height rapidly and bursting into flames before reaching ground. Last seen burning on ground.

iii)   COLOGNE 0148 hrs. 12,000 ft. unidentified A/c seen shot down by flak 10 miles N.W. Not caught in S/Ls. Disintegrated in air.

iv)   COLOGNE 0118 hrs. 14,000 ft. A/C at 16,000 ft seen hit by flak explode in air.

v)   COLOGNE 20 miles W of., C053 hrs. 15,000 ft. A/C seen being attacked by S/E unidentified A/c, burst into flames, crash and explode.

vi)   COLOGNE CC50 hrs. 15,000 ft. A/c seen held in S/L and hit by flak. Fell straight down leaving a trail of smoke.

vii)   OVERFLAKKEE 0145 hrs. 10,000 ft. A/C seen intercepted by fighters and hit by tracer. Appeared to catch fire and later flames seen on ground.

viii)   SCHOUWEN 0137 hrs. 8,000 ft. tracer seen fired in air and immediately afterwards object crashed in flames.

ix)   COLOGNE 0220 hrs., 11,000 ft. R/Gunner reported 3 parachutes caught in one S/L with light flak firing at two of them.

x)   COLOGNE C112 hrs. 16,500 ft. A/c. seen caught in S/L cone and hit by flak and seen to go down alight.

/ Page 9 .....

Appendix A

Page 9.

EN OBSERVATIONS (Contd:)

3 GROUP. (xi) GYMNICH 0125 hrs. 15,500 ft. A/C seen caught in S/Ls over Cologne and hit by flak. It appeared to explode in mid-air.

    xii) HAARSTEDE. 0030 hrs. 17,000 ft. Two A/c seen in water one in Channel S. of Overflakke, second in bay at Bergen.

    xiii) ARNHEIM. 0212 hrs. 10,500 ft. A/c seen picked up by S/1 at 3000 ft. Fired at by L.F. seen to crash.

    xiv) ANTWERP. 0210 hrs., 12,000 ft. Two A/c caught in cones of S/Ls., both shot down.

4 GROUP.

    i) COLOGNE are 0220 hrs. 14,000 ft. four engined A/C seen held in S/Ls going down in flames.

    ii) COLOGNE area 0155 hrs. 14,000 ft. two A/C apparently in collision, also one shot down.

    iii) COLOGNE. 10 miles N.W. of 0149 hrs. 14,000 ft. A/C seen coned with S/Ls with flak at apex catching fire and hitting ground.

    (iv) COLOGNE area. 0210 hrs. 14,000 ft. A/C illuminated in cone of S/L with flak at apex. A/c. burst into flames, descended slowly.

    v) CAPELLEN area 0230 h.s. 14,000 ft. R/gunner reports tracer seen fired in air, terrific flash and A/C seen to fall to ground and burn.

    vi) COLOGNE area 0158 hrs. 13,500 ft. A/c seen hit by flak, burst into flames, 5 of crew seen to bale out.

    vii) COLOGNE area 0220 hrs. 13,000 ft. A/c seen in cone of S/Ls with flak at apex, exploded in air and fell in flames.

    viii) COLOGNE to N.W. of. 0210 hrs. 14,000 ft. four-engined A/C seen in cone of S/Ls with flak at apex. and A/C losing height rapidly.

    ix) COLOGNE 2 miles N. from centre 0205 hours. 13,500 ft. A/C seen and fired at by light flak, fell in flames and exploded on ground.

    x) ANTWERP vicinity 0113 hrs. 13,000 ft. believed A/C in flames seen to hit ground and explode. No flak or S/L seen.

    xi) Position $51^{\circ}25'$ N. $03^{\circ}15'$ E. 0300 hrs. 14,000 ft. Red glow at sea level directly below own A/C - seen to burn for some minutes.

    xii) GEVENBROICH. 0205 h.s., 14,300 ft. Halifax seen to be attacked by believed Me.110 in the stern and hit in starboard inner engine. Large flash and Halifax disappeared in steep dive.

    xiii) SCHOUWEN N. of 0130 hrs. 13,000 ft. unidentified A/C seen to go down, in flames and burn on beach - No flak seen.

    xiv) COLOGNE area. 0219 hrs. 14,500 ft. A/C coned and shot down in flames by heavy flak.

    xv) ROERMOND - COLOGNE 0140/0210 hrs. 14,500 ft. 3 A/C seen shot down on way in and four on way out, one believed by fighters.

5 GROUP.

    i) COLOGNE 15 miles N.W. of. 0105 hrs. 7,000 ft. A/C seen shot down by fighter.

    ii) Near GOEDEREDE 0240 hrs. 11,000 ft. A/C seen to fall on beach.

    iii) MAASTRICHT 10 miles N. of, 0203 hrs. 9,000 ft. A/C seen falling in flames after being attacked by enemy fighter.

    iv) TURNHOUT 10mE0155 hrs. 1000 ft. A/C seen hit by tracer from fighter and to crash in flames.

/Page 10.

Appendix A

Page 10.

OWN OBSERVATIONS (Contd:-)

5 GROUP. v) COLOGNE 20 miles W. of 0050 hrs. 12,000 ft. (2 A/C seen to collide and fall in flames.

vi) DUISKIRCHEN 0100 hrs. 10,000 ft. A/C seen to break up in the air and crash in two places in flames. Possibly two A/C colliding.

vii) TURNHOUT 10 m.S.E. 0151 hrs. 6300 ft. S/E enemy fighter seen falling in flames and burning on ground.

91 GROUP. i) MAASTRICHT 15 miles N.W. 0157 hrs. 13,000 ft. exchange of fire observed between 2 A/C One. A/C seen to burst into flames and crash.

ii) COLOGNE 0103 hrs. 11,500 ft. A/C seen caught in cone of S/Ls, hit by flak, catch fire and pieces fall off.

iii) EINDHOVEN. 10 m. S.E. 0050 hrs. 10,000 ft. Believed Halifax seen to shoot down S/E E/A. E/A seen to hit ground and explode.

iv) COLOGNE 0125 hrs. 10,000 ft. 4 parachutes seen floating to earth.

v) Position 51 degs. 56' N. 02 deg. 40' E. 0310 hrs. 1000 ft. Dinghy seen by Wellington which climbed to 4000 ft, and obtained a fix after dropping flame float.

vi) Position 51 degs. 35' N. 0310 E. 0305 hrs. 8000 ft. A/C believed Wellington in sea.

vii) COLOGNE 5 miles S.W. of 0105 hrs. 11,0000 ft. 2 Wellingtons seen going down on fire.

viii) COLOGNE 3 miles S.E. of 0120 hrs. 10,000 ft. A/C held in S/L cone up which flak was firing. Shoon to go down in flames.

92 GROUP. 1) AACHEN AND COLOGNE between, 0125 hrs. 9,000 ft. A/C caught in S/Ls shot at by flak and descended in flames.

ii) COLOGNE 0101 hrs. 12,000 ft. A/C seen hit by flak and caught fire.

iii) COLOGNE 0155 hrs. 7000 ft. what appeared to be a collision of 2 A/C.

iv) MUNCHEN GLADBACH. 10 miles S. of 0100 hrs. 14,000 ft. A/C seen attacked by fighter and seen to explode in the air.

v) BEED. 8 miles S. of. 0050 hrs. 10000 ft. A/C seen to crash and burst into flames, tracer seen first at about 8000 ft.

vi) ANTWERP 20 miles E. of. 0205 hrs. 50 ft. Wellington seen flying slowly W. at 500 ft. Our A/C followed and overtook it then turned calling it on R/T. No reply received. Then next seen A/C was pancaking in field and crew were seen to be flashing torches. A/C. was not seen to catch fire. It is thought that crew were O.K.

vii) COLOGNE 10 miles W. of. 0105 hrs. 17,000 ft. our A/C saw another at 12,0000 ft. attacked by fighters (tracer seen) A/c caught fire and blew up in air.

viii) ANTWERP 10 miles E. of. 0152 hrs. 7000 ft. S/E A/C seen to burst into flames and crash as a result of exchange of fire, with believed four engined bomber.

In addition to the above there were over one hundred other observations of A/C seen shot down on route and over the target.

10. ENEMY CLAIMS/OWN LOSSES.

Enemy claims.

British Bombers carried out terrorist raids on the inner city of Cologne. Night fighters and A.A. artillery   /shot

Appendix A

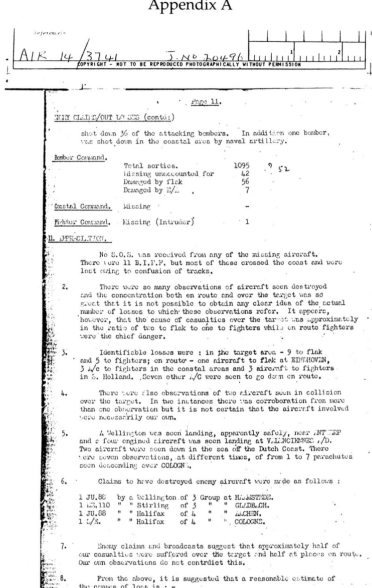

Page 11.

ENEMY CLAIMS/OUR LOSSES (contd:)

shot down 36 of the attacking bombers. In addition one bomber, was shot down in the coastal area by naval artillery.

Bomber Command.

Total sorties.	1095	9 52
Missing unaccounted for	42	
Damaged by flak	56	
Damaged by E/A.	7	

Coastal Command.   Missing   -

Fighter Command.   Missing (Intruder)   1

11. APPRECIATION.

No S.O.S. was received from any of the missing aircraft. There were 11 B.I.F.F. but most of these crossed the coast and were lost owing to confusion of tracks.

2.   There were so many observations of aircraft seen destroyed and the concentration both en route and over the target was so great that it is not possible to obtain any clear idea of the actual number of losses to which these observations refer. It appears, however, that the cause of casualties over the target was approximately in the ratio of two to flak to one to fighters while en route fighters were the chief danger.

3.   Identifiable losses were : in the target area – 9 to flak and 5 to fighters; en route – one aircraft to flak at EINDHOVEN, 3 A/c to fighters in the coastal areas and 3 aircraft to fighters in S. Holland. Seven other A/C were seen to go down en route.

4.   There were also observations of two aircraft seen in collision over the target. In two instances there was corroboration from more than one observation but it is not certain that the aircraft involved were necessarily our own.

5.   A Wellington was seen landing, apparently safely, near ANT ERP and a four engined aircraft was seen landing at VALENCIENNES A/D. Two aircraft were seen down in the sea off the Dutch Coast. There were seven observations, at different times, of from 1 to 7 parachutes seen descending over COLOGNE.

6.   Claims to have destroyed enemy aircraft were made as follows :

1 JU.88	by a	Wellington	of 3	Group	at	HAAMSTEDE.
1 ME.110	"	" Stirling	of 3	"	"	GLADBACH.
1 JU.88	"	" Halifax	of 4	"	"	AACHEN.
1 E/A.	"	" Halifax	of 4	"	"	COLOGNE.

7.   Enemy claims and broadcasts suggest that approximately half of our casualties were suffered over the target and half at places en route. Our own observations do not contradict this.

8.   From the above, it is suggested that a reasonable estimate of the causes of loss is : -

12 aircraft to flak of which the majority were lost over the target. ⎫
16 aircraft to night fighters over the target.   ⎪
10 aircraft to night fighters en route.   ⎬ 52
4 aircraft possibly due to collision with other aircraft.   ⎪
10 aircraft to 'causes unknown'   ⎭

H.Q. B.C.,
AIR STAFF (INT.3)
BC/S. 24648/1/Ops. 1 (a)

Issued at 1830 hours 6th June 1942.

xii

Appendix A

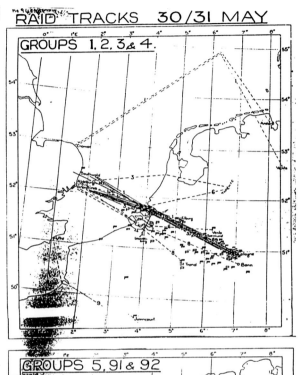

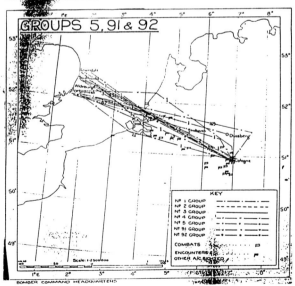

Appendix B

War Room, A.M.

NIGHT RAIDING/ATTACK REPORT NO. 97/43.

NIGHT 16/17th MAY, 1943.

FILE No. ....
TO .... ON ....

1. MAIN TARGETS.

	Group	Aircraft Despatched	Attacked Target	E/A Attacked	E/A Enc.	Other A/C Seen	Missing
MOEHNE DAM SORPE DAM EDER DAM SCHWELM DAM	5	19 (LANC)	15	-	-	-	8

2. OTHER TARGETS.

BERLIN	2	3 (MOS)	2	-	-	-	-
DUSSELDORF	2	2 (MOS)	2	-	-	-	-
MUNSTER	2	2 (MOS)	2	-	-	-	-
COLOGNE	2	2 (MOS)	2	-	-	-	-
MINELAYING	3	13 (STIR) 2 (LANC)	13 2	-	-	1	-
MINELAYING	4	16 (WELL.)	16	-	-	-	1
MINELAYING	6	21 (WELL.)	20	-	-	-	-
LEAFLETS ORLEANS	92	1 (WELL.) 3 (WELL.IKI)	1 3	-	-	-	-

3. BOMBING PARTICULARS.

	Group	Time	Average bombing height	Average bomb load per A/C.
MOEHNE DAM SORPE DAM EDER DAM SCHWELM DAM	5	0023-0049 0046-0514 0052-0139 0337	60. ft.	1 mine

4. OTHER TARGETS.

	Group	Time	Average bombing height	Average bomb load per A/C.
BERLIN	2	0114-0118	21,000 ft.	2,000 lbs.
DUSSELDORF	2	0005-0007	24,000 ft.	2,000 lbs.
MUNSTER	2	0013-0016	25,000 ft.	2,000 lbs.
COLOGNE	2	0005-0012	25,500 ft.	2,000 lbs.
MINELAYING	3	0256-0330 0300-0305	800 ft. 800 ft.	9 A/C 6 mines 4 A/C 5 mines 6 mines
MINELAYING	4	0032-0153	800 ft.	2 mines
MINELAYING	6	0253-0326	2,500 ft.	2 mines
LEAFLETS ORLEANS	92	0132 0121-0223	15,000 ft. 15,000 ft.	/

/Page 2....

Appendix B

- 2 -

5.   ROUTES.

For routes taken see route map.

W.H.2.

Ruhr.   Small amounts of cloud.   Moderate to good visibility.

Berlin.   7-8/10ths thin cloud, tops 10,000 ft.   Some ground haze.

Routes.   Small amounts of cloud, mainly high.   Moderate to good
visibility.

Bay of Biscay.   Little or no cloud.   Good visibility.

Moon.   Three quarters full.

7.   ENCOUNTERS/OTHER A/C SEEN.

3 Group.   i)   5400N. 0430E. 0300 hrs. 1,500 ft.   Unidentified E/A with white
light.

8.   FLAK/SEARCHLIGHTS/OTHER AIDS TO DEFENCE.

General.   Low flying aircraft were subjected to light flak fire from
several points on route, notably between BOCHOLT and BORKEN where about 50 S/Ls
each with 2 light guns were reported in addition to light guns on the railway at
at LUDINGHAUSEN where the DORTMUND-EMS CANAL was defended with S/Ls and light guns
the MOHNE dam was defended by light guns from the towers on the dam.

Aircraft flying at 22/23,000 ft. report accurate heavy flak at MUNSTER,
DUSSELDORF and STADL.

9.   WIRELESS INTELLIGENCE.

64 sorties by controlled night fighters were heard.   Nine of these were
operating against British aircraft.

2.   Two attempted interceptions and one indecisive combat were heard but
there were no claims.

3.   British aircraft were reported flying very low in the KOBLENZ area at
0220 hrs.

10.   ENEMY CLAIMS/OWN LOSSES.

Enemy claims.   "Weak forces of the R.A.F. penetrated into Reich territory.
Two dams were damaged.   8 of the attacking A/C were shot down and 9 further A/C
destroyed over occupied Western territories, including one brought down by
formations of the Army."

Bomber Command.

	Dams	Other targets	Total
Sorties	19	67	86
Missing unaccounted for	8	1	9
Damaged by flak	4	-	4
Damaged by E/A	-	-	-

Coastal Command.   Missing   -

Fighter Command.   Missing (Intruder)   1

11.   APPRECIATION.

Three of the eight missing aircraft on dams in W. GERMANY were heard
after attacking their targets but no indication was given of the cause of loss.

/Page 3.....

XV

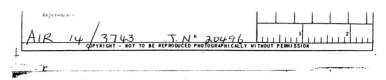

- 3 -

2.   From individual observations of other aircraft it appears
that three A/C were lost on the way out to the target, one to light
flak at TEXEL, one to light flak near IOKSTEN and a third possibly
in the HELIGICH area.   Two aircraft were lost in the target areas,
one to light flak at HOHLD and another at SOMLD probably as a result
of damage sustained in the explosion of its own mine.   There were
further observations of aircraft apparently shot down, after leaving
the target, near HULL and TILBURY.   The cause of loss was not stated.

3.   Four of the eleven aircraft which returned from the attacks
on the dams were damaged, three by light flak and one by M/G.

4.   No sightings of E/A were reported and there is no evidence
that any losses were due to night fighters.

5.   Nothing is known of the missing minelayer of 4 Group.

6.   Causes of loss may be estimated as: one A/C due to the
explosion of its own mine, at least three A/C to light flak and one
A/C - the missing minelayer - to "causes unknown".   The remaining
four missing aircraft were probably all lost owing to light flak.

H.Q.B.C.
AIR STAFF.
BC/S.27376/Int.3.
Issued at 1800 hrs. 22nd May, 1943.

Appendix B

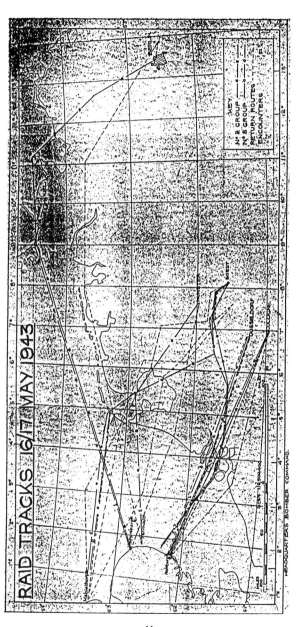

Appendix C

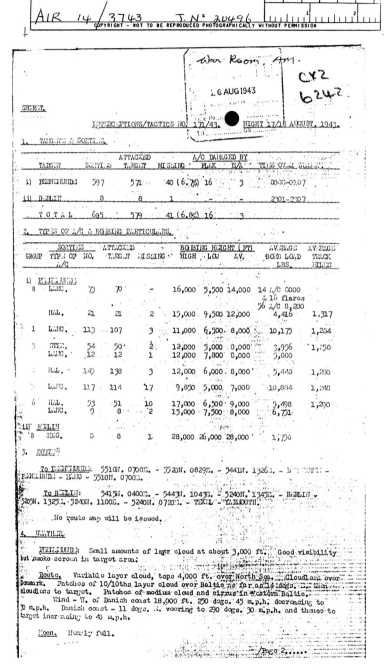

War Room, A.M.

26 AUG 1943

CX2
624.?

SECRET.

INTERCEPTIONS/TACTICS NO. 171/43.   NIGHT 17/18 AUGUST, 1943.

1. TARGETS & SORTIES.

TARGET	SORTIES	ATTACKED TARGET	MISSING	A/C DAMAGED BY FLAK	E/A	TIME OVER TARGET
i) PEENEMUNDE	597	571	40 (6.7%)	16	3	0000-0107
ii) BERLIN	8	8	1	-	-	2301-2307
TOTAL	605	579	41 (6.8%)	16	3	

2. TYPES OF A/C & BOMBING PARTICULARS.

GROUP	TYPE OF A/C	SORTIES NO.	ATTACKED TARGET	MISSING	BOMBING HEIGHT (FT) HIGH	LOW	AV.	AVERAGE BOMB LOAD LBS.	AVERAGE TRACK MILES
i) PEENEMUNDE									
8	LANC.	73	70	-	16,000	5,500	14,000	14 A/C 0000 & 16 flares 56 A/C 8,200	
	HAL.	21	21	2	15,000	9,500	12,000	4,416	1,317
1	LANC.	113	107	3	11,000	6,500	8,000	10,175	1,284
3	STIR.	54	50	2	12,000	5,000	8,000	3,956	1,750
	LANC.	12	12	1	12,000	7,800	8,000	5,000	
	HAL.	145	138	3	12,000	6,000	8,000	5,443	1,200
	LANC.	117	114	17	9,850	5,000	7,000	10,884	1,248
6	HAL.	53	51	10	17,000	6,500	9,000	5,498	1,290
	LANC.	9	8	2	15,000	7,500	8,000	6,751	
ii) BERLIN									
8	MOS.	8	8	1	28,000	26,000	28,000	1,750	

3. ROUTES.

To PEENEMUNDE: 5510N. 0700E. - 5520N. 0829E. - 5441N. 1326E. - D.R. ROUTE - PEENEMUNDE - INNO - 5510N. 0700E.

To BERLIN: 5415N. 0400E. - 5443N. 1043E. - 5240N. 1345E. - BERLIN - 5205N. 1325E. - 5240N. 1100E. - 5240N. 0720E. - TEXEL - YARMOUTH.

No route map will be issued.

4. WEATHER.

PEENEMUNDE: Small amounts of layer cloud at about 3,000 ft. Good visibility but smoke screen in target area.

Route. Variable layer cloud, tops 4,000 ft. over North Sea. Cloudless over Denmark. Patches of 10/10ths layer cloud over Baltic as far as 14 idegs. E. then cloudless to target. Patches of medium cloud and cirrus in Western Baltic.
Wind - W. of Danish coast 18,000 ft. 250 degs. 45 m.p.h. decreasing to 30 m.p.h. Danish coast - 11 degs. E. veering to 290 degs. 30 m.p.h. and thence to target increasing to 40 m.p.h.

Moon. Nearly full.

/Page 2......

Appendix C

Reference:-

AIR 14/3743 I.N° 20496

- 2 -

5. COMBATS & E/A ENCOUNTERED.

8 Group. i) KARLSRUHE. 5 m. N.E. 0053 hrs. 9,000 ft. Lancaster sighted T/E E/A 100 ft. below to starboard. R/G fired 4 short rounds and M/U/G 3 bursts. E/A broke away to starboard, crossed in front of Lancaster to port and was lost. No return of fire.

1 Group. i) 5445N. 1225E. 0015 hrs. 10,000 ft. JU.88 seen 500 yds. on port quarter down. Lancaster made diving turn to port, M/U/G fired 2-3 secs. burst. E/A broke away from 350-400 yds. on starboard quarter up, and not seen again.

ii) SASNITZ. 5 m. W. 0024 hrs. 8,000 ft. ME.110 seen 500 yds. star... beam. Lancaster turned to starboard, maintaining height, and R/G fired short bu... E/A turned to port and was lost.

iii) KARLSRUHE. 0037 hrs. 8,000 ft. T/E A/C approached 600 ft. be... from starboard to port quarter 800 yds. R/G fired 20 rounds at 800 yds; E/A... pooled off. Lancaster dived to port and E/A disappeared.

iv) KARLSRUHE. 0041 hrs. 8,000 ft. T/E A/C approached from starbo... to port quarter 800 yds., 500 ft. below. Lancaster dived to port, R/G fired 10 ... rounds and E/A pooled off to starboard.

v) KARLSRUHE. 0042 hrs. 7,500 ft. ME.109 seen port quarter, 1000 y... attacking another Lancaster, firing two bursts. E/A came round on... own 500-600 yds. astern of our A/C which took weaving action, E/A fired 2 bursts, ... tracer passing immediately beneath Lancaster. R/G fired one long and one short burst. Flames seen coming from engine of E/A which broke away and fell with flames pouring from engine and continued burning on ground after explosion. ME.109 claimed as destroyed.

vi) HUSUM. 10 m. N.W. 0100 hrs. 17,000 ft. Believed ME.109 approached from port quarter below to about 200 yds. opening fire at this range with 2 short bursts. Lancaster dived to port and R/G replied with one short burst. M/U/G at 300 yds. range fired 300 rounds claiming strikes in vicinity of nose and cockpit. E/A immediately broke away to port.

vii) 5423N. 1200E. 0104 hrs. 18,000 ft. E/A approaching 1,500 yds. dead astern same height, closed to 6/800 yds. Lancaster made diving turn to starboard and R/G fired 3 secs. burst. E/A broke away to port and not seen again.

viii) 5446N. 0746E. 0105 hrs. 16,000 ft. JU.88 approached dead astern, R/G and M/U/G opened fire simultaneously at 500 yds. range. E/A closed to 250 yds. firing one long burst and then pooled off to starboard. Lancaster had meanwhile dived to port. E/A orbitted and again approached from dead astern to 350 yds. firing cannon. Lancaster corkscrewed to port. M/U/G fired 700 rounds in 3 bursts and R/G a similar number. Engagement lasted 5 mins. and E/A then dived steeply to starboard; flame was seen in neighbourhood of where E/A disappeared, falling rapidly towards sea. E/A claimed as probably destroyed.

3 Group. i) PEENEMUNDE. 0220 hrs. 7,500 ft. E/A came in to 400 yds. from green quarter with guns firing. M/U/G fired a burst and Stirling corkscrewed. E/A broke away to port and R/G fired burst as E/A disappeared.

ii) 5413N. 1307E. 0036 hrs. 10,000 ft. HE.210 came in to 600 yds. dead astern. R/G opened fire, E/A broke off to port and disappeared.

iii) 5456N. 0638E. 2250 hrs. 8,000 ft. Stirling fired at by FW.190 from astern. R/G fired short burst.

iv) 5317N. 0231E. 2250 hrs. 5,000 ft. Stirling attacked by 2 JU.88's. One E/A opened fire. Stirling replied and strike was seen.

v) BRACOBING. 5 m. N.E. 0001 hrs. 11,000 ft. Stirling and 2 DO.217's one of which passed in front, the second Dornier seen on green quarter. R/G and M/U/G opened fire and, strikes were seen. E/A dived steeply and hit ground in flames. One E/A claimed destroyed.

vi) PEENEMUNDE. 0016 hrs. 8,000 ft. JU.88 approached from astern and fired one burst. Stirling replied.

vii) MARIENDYK. 0120 hrs. 11,000 ft. FW.190 approached and R/G fired burst. E/A continued to approach and R/G fired further burst.

/Page 3.....

Appendix C

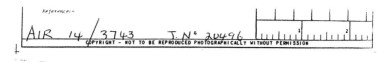
- 3 -

4 Group.

i) SLT N. 2318 hrs. 14,000 ft. JU.88 first seen on starboard quarter coming in to attack. Halifax turned in to attack. E/A turned away and held off. Halifax made corkscrew dive. R/G gave 3 secs. burst at about 300 yds. E/A broke off on starboard beam, not seen again.

ii) LANDO ISLAND. 15 m. W. 2316 hrs. 14,000 ft. DO.217 approached about 1,000 yds. astern, dropped a reddish flare and then crossed over to green closing to about 800 yds. MU/G fired 2 short bursts and E/A continued to green and disappeared.

iii) PEENEMUNDE. 0017 hrs. 8,000 ft. ME.110 on port quarter up crossed to starb'ard at 600 yds. R/G gave short burst, Halifax corkscrewed to starboard and lost E/A.

iv) 5437N. 1045E. 0124 hrs. 12,000 ft. S/E E/A came in on port bow and was fired at by another Halifax on starboard bow. E/A dived to our starboard bow and MU/G fired a burst. E/A moved round beam to starboard quarter and came in to attack. At 600 yds, R/G opened fire. Own A/C made diving turn to starboard. E/A did not open fire and was lost.

v) LANGELAND. 0117 hrs. 12,000 ft. JU.88 seen at 400 yds. on port side. Halifax made diving turn to port and passed under E/A, R/G firing a second burst. E/A lost.

vi) RUDEN ISLAND. 0027 hrs. 8,000 ft. JU.88 came in from port above and opened fire; R/G and MU/G replied. A Halifax came in between and protected. Combat abandoned and E/A disappeared.

vii) PEENEMUNDE. 12,000 ft. 0025 hrs. ME.109 attacked from starboard quarter, opened fire at 300 yds. and then broke away. Halifax opened fire with 200 rounds - slight evasive action turning into attack.

viii) 5415N. 1328E. 13,000 ft. 0045hrs. JU.88 came in from starboard quarter up. First seen at 400 yds., crossed tail at 200 yds, climbed on to port quarter and disappeared. R/G fired at E/A from 400 yds. until disappeared. E/A did not return fire.

ix) 5510N. 0700E. 9,000 ft. 0214 hrs. JU.88 passed astern from port to starboard and at 300 yds. R/G fired a burst which appeared to hit port engine. E/A continued to follow. Halifax until evaded by diving turn to port.

x) N. Point of FALSTER. 2000 hrs. 13,000 ft. Another Halifax seen to starboard and below, corkscrewing. R/G then sighted a JU.88 at 6/700 yds. on port quarter approaching our Halifax. When the JU.88 had closed to 700 yds. our Halifax made diving turn to port and commenced to corkscrewed. The JU.88 followed our A/C and opened fire at 700 yds., As Halifax was making starboard turn on corkscrew. Our A/C was hit by E/A fire in fore part of fuselage and the flight engineer was wounded in foot. Our A/C turned to port and the JU.88 was lost to sight. Coming back on track our A/C passed across the stern of the other Halifax at about 800 yds. distance whereupon the R/G of the other Halifax opened fire on our A/C but missed.

xi) GREIFSWALD. 8 m. NNE. 7,500 ft. 0035 hrs. FW.190 seen on starboard quarter down, at 500 yds. Halifax started corkscrew immediately to starboard, opening fire at 350 yds., both gunners claiming hits. E/A did not return fire but broke away to port quarter up 200 yds. away.

xii) GREIFSWALD. 10 m. NNW. 0040 hrs. 9,500 ft. Believed ME.110 seen on port quarter up, passing over to starboard/down, when it opened fire at 400 yds. range. Halifax started to corkscrew to starboard and R/G opened fire at 600 yds. claiming hits. E/A broke away to port quarter and repeated attack, finally breaking away to port quarter.

xiii) GREIFSWALD. 10 m. NW. 10,000 ft. 0041 hrs. Another Halifax seen on starboard quarter half down which crossed underneath and reappeared on port bow 200 ft. up; putting its nose down, it did a diving turn to port. Levelling out on port bow, flying on a parallel course to our A/C at 300 yds., it then did a steep turn to starboard. Opening fire from dead astern it disappeared to starboard beam and was finally lost to sight astern.

xiv) 5500N. 0700E. 0305 hrs. 11,000 ft. JU.88 approached from about 100 yds. to starboard, same level, and closed in to 700 yds. R/G gave instructions for diving turn to starboard. E/A tried to turn away to port and got caught in our slipstream. E/A turned right over and R/G gave one 2 secs. burst at about 400 yds. E/A went in to cloud apparently endeavouring to gain control. Just after E/A disappeared two red Verey lights were fired from sea at about 3 mins. intervals.

/Page 4......

XX

Appendix C

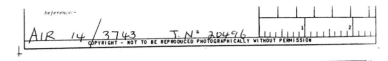

- 4 -

GROUP. i) PEENEMUNDE Area. 0059 hrs. 7,000 ft. ME.110 seen silhouetted against cloud in light part of sky on starboard quarter above. E/A approached in curve of pursuit. R/G fired short burst at 500 yds. then guns jammed. Lancaster made diving turn to starboard followed by a corkscrew. R/G fired as E/A closed to 200 yds., strikes being observed on nose and cabin of E/A which broke away to port and was not seen again.

ii) 5520N. 0829E. 2347 hrs. 18,300 ft. JU.88 seen astern and above. Lancaster corkscrewed and R/G fired one long burst. E/A broke away and was not seen again.

iii) PEENEMUNDE. 0048 hrs. 6,000 ft. Lancaster was fired on by ME.109 which approached from astern and above. R/G and H/U/G returned fire and E/A broke away and was not seen again.

iv) PEENEMUNDE. 20 m. W. 0055 hrs. 6,000 ft. Lancaster attacked by FW.190 which approached from starboard quarter. Fire from E/A was returned by H/U/G and R/G as Lancaster went into corkscrew. Combat lasted 11 mins. Somthing seen on E/A and when E/A broke away to starboard it was seen to be on fire. An A/C was seen to burst into flames about 25 to 30 miles west of target at 0105 hrs; thought to be this E/A.

v) PEENEMUNDE. 0048 hrs. 5/600 ft. 2 A/C seen to starboard bow 1,000 ft. above. First definitely identified as Lancaster. The second approached rapidly from astern and assumed to be a fighter. Pilot ordered H/U/G and F/G to open fire on assumed fighter and simultaneously forward tracer seen from nose of this A/C. First A/C (Lancaster) went down in shallow dive but not seen to crash. Our A/C manoeuvred under second A/C (assumed fighter) and F/G fired 3 long bursts while H/U/G fired about 50 rounds. Tracer passed below A/C which broke away to port and was then seen to be 4-engined and twin ruddered (believed Lancaster).

vi) PEENEMUNDE. 0050 hrs. 7,000 ft. JU.88 (grey) passed from starboard to port, below, about 200 yds away. H/U/G opened fire, result unobserved. No defensive manoeuvre as Lancaster on bombing run.

vii) 5436N. 1226E. 0107 hrs. 11,000 ft. T/E E/A on port quarter down sighted at about 700 yds. E/A came in and Lancaster did diving turn to port. H/U/G and R/G both fired 100 rounds and E/A disappeared from view. E/A carried white light in nose which was switched off when E/A attacked.

viii) PEENEMUNDE. 0057 hrs. 6,400 ft. JU.88 approached from dead astern and above. R/G and H/U/G gave one sec. burst at 1100 yds. E/A did not attack.

ix) 5417N. 0310E. 0058 hrs. 6,000 ft. T/E E/A with light in nose appeared about 500 yds away on port quarter. E/A then approached from port beam and port quarter. H/U/G and R/G opened fire and E/A replied. Lancaster did diving turn to port and E/A broke away to starboard. E/A approached again 2 mins. later from port quarter 500 yds. Both gunners gave short burst and E/A replied. Lancaster started diving turn to port. Strikes appeared to enter nose of E/A, nose light went out and a red glow appeared which was seen to fall and turn on ground. E/A claimed as destroyed.

x) PEENEMUNDE. 0100 hrs. 8,500 ft. JU.88 first seen 200 yds port side, H/U/G fired continuously until E/A dead astern, R/G also fired and tracer seen striking E/A which broke away 300 yds on port quarter. E/A did not open fire. Lancaster on bombing run and no evasive action taken.

xi) 5427N. 1240E. 0110 hrs. 9,000 ft. ME.109 on port quarter, 150 yds. opened fire damaging Lancaster and wounding R/G. H/U/G fired one burst and saw strikes on E/A which broke away on starboard quarter. JU.88 seen just previous to attack. Lancaster corkscrewed.

xii) 5510N. 0710E. 0237 hrs. 12,000 ft. ME.210 seen at 1,000 yds, port bow, slightly below. E/A closed to port, port quarter, Lancaster made diving turn to port, and at 500 yds. R/G opened fire. E/A broke away to starboard without firing and not seen again.

xiii) 5503N. 1005E. 2357 hrs. 17,000 ft. JU.88 sighted 950 yds. astern, E/A turned upwards and inwards from port quarter. At about 800 yds R/G and H/U/G fired 150 rounds, and E/A peeled off to starboard.

xiv) LUCEN ISLAND. 0129 hrs. 15,000 ft. T/E E/A sighted 1,000 ft. below, and Lancaster started weaving. E/A climbed on starboard quarter, Lancaster made diving turn to starboard, and E/A followed. Both gunners got in good bursts and E/A blew up at about 400 yds. E/A claimed destroyed.

xv) STRALSUND. 0053 hrs. 13,000 ft. ME.109 approached from starboard quarter below, firing from 800 yds and hitting Lancaster, which made diving turn to starboard and weaved in dark part of sky. R/G fired approx. 600 rounds, and E/A lost.

/Page 5....

xxi

Appendix C

- 5 -

xvi) 5430N. 1250E. 0100 hrs. 10,000 ft. ME.110 approached from starboard quarter below and fired two bursts. Lancaster made diving turn to starboard and corkscrewed into dark sky. M/U/G fired approx. 100 rounds, and E/A lost.

xvii) FLENSBURG, 0106 hrs. 5,700 ft. ME.110 painted white made several approaches but did not fire. Lancaster opened fire from 600 yds., and took corkscrew evasive action throughout encounter.

Group. i) FLENSBURG area, 0048 hrs. 8,000 ft. ME.110 approached from astern below, to about 400 yds. Halifax made diving turn to starboard, E/A followed and again closed to 400 yds. R/G fired several bursts followed by several bursts from M/U/G. Tracer hit front part of E/A which climbed to port and glided off without opening fire. E/A was seen to be on fire before disappearing.

ii) FLENSBURG 0052 hrs. 8,000 ft. Halifax approached from astern and below by ME.110 at 460 yds. Halifax corkscrewed and fired long burst. E/A climbed to about 500 yds astern and opened fire. M/U/G and R/G replied and continued firing which was returned by E/A. Tracer from Halifax was seen to be hitting fuselage of E/A which stopped firing, broke away to starboard and was lost.

iii) RUGEN ISLAND, S. end, 0046 hrs. 6,000 ft. Halifax attacked four times from port and starboard astern by ME.109 with cannon and machine-gun fire. M/U/G and R/G replied and shot E/A down at the end of the combat.

6. FLAK/SEARCHLIGHTS/OTHER AIDS TO DEFENCE.

Peenemunde. Slight heavy flak firing a barrage at about 10,000 ft. towards the end of the attack. Slight to moderate light flak in the target area but very few S/Ls. A smoke screen was in operation but did not develop fully until the later part of the attack.

General. Very little flak opposition was encountered on the route but heavy flak of varying intensity was seen from defended areas off the route, notably FLENSBURG where it was reported as accurate and intense with S/L co-operation. The defences of KIEL and WILHELM were also active.

Balloons were seen at FLENSBURG at about 10,000 ft.

7. WIRELESS INTELLIGENCE.

Thirty-eight controlled night fighters were heard between 2041 and 0230 hrs. but of these only five were heard active against hostile aircraft.

Twenty-eight uncontrolled night fighter patrols were also heard in the same period. Hostile aircraft were reported in various localities from N. of AHLAND and BORKUM through WESTERLAND to ROSTOCK, STETTIN and SWINEMUNDE.

An attack in force on BERLIN was evidently expected and aircraft from many night fighter units in Western Germany were heard landing at airfields in the BERLIN area and to the north west, including STAAKEN, BRANDENBURG, STENDAL, BRECHIN, NEUBRANDENBURG, and GREIFSWALD.

In all, the estimated fighter effort by the G.A.F. is about 110 aircraft.

Owing to the distance and the nature of the traffic no complete record of claims, if any, could be obtained. One reference to three victories in the SLT/S.DENMARK area was all that was heard.

8. ENEMY CLAIMS.

Last night the enemy dropped a large number of H.E. and I.Bs. on localities in the coastal area of N.GERMANY. Night fighters and A.A. guns of the Luftwaffe shot down at least 37 British bombers.

9. APPRECIATION.

Nothing was heard from the forty-one missing aircraft.

Very considerable activity by enemy night fighters was heard during the operation. While it was apparent that this activity was planned in anticipation of an attack on Berlin which resulted in a part of the effort being spent over the area

/Page 6....

Appendix C

- 6 -

between Berlin and the Baltic coast numerous fighters were operating over the route from the Danish coast to the target. Orthodox methods of night fighter control were not greatly in evidence and most aircraft were free-lancing in co-operation with a running commentary from ground stations. Weather conditions were favourable for this type of operation and it is probable that the majority of our losses were suffered as a result of this technique.

3.   Early arrivals over the target report little heavy or light flak but later in the attack an increase in light flak was reported and some casualties resulted.   Observations of other aircraft suggest that a total of seven bombers were lost to flak in the target area.

4.   Losses to flak on the route were seen at HANO both on the outward and homeward journeys when aircraft were coned and shot down.   Other flak losses were apparently due to aircraft straying over well-defended areas notably at HAMBURG where two aircraft were shot down on the way home and SYLT where another was lost on the way to the target.

5.   Losses to fighters on the route, according to observations, occurred at HANO (2 A/C), KIEL, STRALSUND, and FLENSBURG.   In the target area there were a possible six further aircraft shot down.

6.   Five claims to have destroyed E/A were made, a Do.217 by a Stirling of 3 Group, ME.109's by a Lancaster of 1 Group and a Halifax of 6 Group and two T/E E/A's by Lancasters of 5 Group.

7.   There is no information about the P.F. Mosquito missing on BERLIN.

8.   Causes of loss, so far as they can be estimated are: 14 A/C to flak and 11 A/C to night fighters.   This gives an incomplete picture of the losses as a whole and it is thought that the majority of those not otherwise accounted for were probably shot down by fighters.   A ratio of 2 A/C lost to fighters for every one to flak is probably a more accurate estimate but no definite figures can be given.

H. Q. B. C.
AIR STAFF.
BC/S.27876/Int.3.
Issued at 1200 hrs. 25th August, 1943.

Appendix D

A.M.W.R.

20 NOV 1944   5/HQ9570

UY 27 03 16
SECRET.

INTERCEPTIONS/TACTICS NO. 286/44.   DAY, 18th NOVEMBER, and
NIGHT, 18th/19th NOVEMBER 1944.

PART I - DAY, 18th NOVEMBER.

1. TARGETS & SORTIES.

TARGET	GROUP	TYPE OF A/C	SORTIES	ATTACKED TARGET	MISSING	HEIGHT 000' ft	TIME OVER TARGET
i) MUNSTER	4,6,8		477	443	1 -	15-28	1455-1516
	4	HAL.	211	195	-	15-20	1504-1516
	6	HAL.	156	152)	-	15-18	1455-1513
		LANC	44	43)			
	8	LANC	50	50	-	15½-18½	1456-1513
		MOS.	18	3	-	28	1458-1507
ii) SIGNALS PATROLS	100	HAL.	4	3	-		
iii) MET. RECCE.	8	MOS.	1	1	-		
TOTAL			484	447	-		

2. APPRECIATION.

This was a sky-marking attack on the town of Munster, which put up nothing like the opposition that its Heavy Flak guns (estimated at 80) could have fired given clear weather. There was 10/10ths 3c, up to 8,000ft and the bombers attacked from low 10/10ths Cirrus which was at 18-20,000ft. There was a wind of 60 mph from the W.W.

The force flew down wind almost direct from the Belgian coast, skirting the north of the Ruhr defences with very little opposition, though the Battle area round Emmerich, Cleve, Bocholt and Wesel produced slight predicted flak on the homeward journey. Of 211 Halifaxes of No.4 Group not one was damaged.

As usual the formation keeping appeared, to the fighter escort, better on the approach than on withdrawal. The enemy was able to keep the bombers plotted continuously to their target and part way back, but no fighters reacted. There were 30 S/E fighters active in the area between Venlo and Euskirchen at the time of this attack but these seem to have been engaged on close support of German troops.

The crew of one Halifax baled out near Antwerp. On return frontal cloud covered part of Yorkshire where cloud base was low in light rain and visibility poor. Two aircraft collided when circling over neighbouring bases.

3. ROUTE AND TIMING ORDERED.

Munster. Orfordness - Blankenburg - 5143N 0639E - Munster - 5205N 0735E - 5205N 0700E - 5130N 0600E - Blankenburg - Orfordness.
T.O.T. 1450-1520hrs. Over Continent 1405-1630 hrs.

No route map will be issued.

PART II - NIGHT 18th/19th NOVEMBER.

1. TARGETS & SORTIES.

TARGET	GROUP	TYPE OF A/C	SORTIES	ATTACKED TARGET	MISSING	HEIGHT 000 ft	TIME OVER TARGET
i) WANNE EICKEL	1,8		309	295	1 (.3%)	12½-22	1852-1908
	1	LANC	253	252	1	16-19½	1859-1908
	8	LANC	32	32	-	12½-19½	1856-1906
		MOS.	24	11	-	21-22	1852-1900
ii) WIESBADEN (Spoof)	8	MOS.	31	30	-	22½-27	1846-1907
iii) HANNOVER	8	MOS.	21	18	-	22-26½	1850-1855
iv) ERFURT	8	MOS.	6	3	-	29½-30	2003-2010
v) BOMBER SUPPORT	100	M,S,H,F,Lib.	67	61	-		
vi) SIGNALS PATROLS	100	H,W.	6	4	-		
TOTAL			440	411	1 (.2%)		

/Page 2.....

xxiv

Appendix E

SECRET.

INTERCEPTIONS/TACTICS NO. 71.   NIGHT 30/31 MARCH, 1944.

1. TARGETS & SORTIES.

	TARGET	SORTIES	ATTACKED TARGET	MISSING	A/C DAMAGED BY FLAK	E/A	TIME OVER TARGET
(i)	NURNBERG	795	710	94 (11.8%)	15	31	0103 - 0139
(ii)	AACHEN	6	5				2354 - 0034
(iii)	COLOGNE	9	7				2257 - 0009
(iv)	KASSEL	19	19				0024 - 0030
(v)	DORTMUND	1	1				2123
(vi)	JULLANADORP	2	1				2305
(vii)	OBERHAUSEN	3	1		1		2123
(viii)	A/F'S IN HOLLAND	11	8				2220 - 2340
(ix)	MINELAYING	55	54				2323 - 0343
(x)	LEAFLETS	8	8				2111 - 2228
(xi)	FIGHTER PATROLS	19	15		1	1	
(xii)	SPECIAL OPERATIONS	22		1 (4.5%)			
	T O T A L	960	829	95 (10%)	16	32	

2. TYPES OF A/C & BOMBING PARTICULARS.

GROUP	TYPE OF A/C	SORTIES NO.	ATTACKED TARGET	MISSING	BOMBING HEIGHT (FT). HIGH	LOW	AV.	AVERAGE BOMB LOAD LBS.	AVERAGE TRACK MILES
(i)	NURNBERG.								
	8 LANC.	110	106	11	21,000	15,000	19,000	8,731 & fl.	1,334
	MOS.	9	8	-	25,000	24,000	24,000	1,944	
	1 LANC.	180	164	21	24,000	16,000	22,000	10,385	1,430
	3 LANC.	56	47	8	24,000	15,000	21,000	8,826	1,300
	4 HAL.III	121	98	20	23,000	18,000	21,000	3,610	1,526
	5 LANC.	201	180	21	23,000	17,000	21,000	9,543	1,411
	6 HAL.III	93	83	10	23,000	19,000	21,000	3,469	1,582
	LANC.	25	24	3	22,000	19,000	21,000	6,769	1,582
(ii)	AACHEN.								
	8 MOS.	6	5	-	30,000	27,000	29,000	1,750	
(iii)	KASSEL.								
	8 MOS.	19	19	-	25,000	20,000	24,000	2,513	
(iv)	DORTMUND.								
	8 MOS.	1	1	-	-	-	30,000	4,000	
(v)	JULIANADORP.								
	8 MOS.	2	1	-	-	-	28,000	2,000	
(vi)	OBERHAUSEN.								
	8 MOS.	3	1	-	-	-	30,000	4,000	
(vii)	A/F'S IN HOLLAND.								
	8 MOS.	11	8	-	32,000	27,000	30,000	1,500 & fl.	
(viii)	MINELAYING.								
	3 STIR.	6	6	-	2,500	1,000	2,000	6 mines.	
	4 HAL.	20	19	-	14,500	13,400	14,000	2 mines.	
	6 HAL.	29	29	-	15,000	14,600	14,800	? mines.	

/Page 2.

Appendix E

- 2 -

GROUP	SORTIES TYPE OF A/C	NO.	ATTACKED TARGET	MISSING	BOMBING HEIGHT (FT) HIGH	LOW	AV.	AVERAGE BOMB LOAD LBS.	AVERAGE TRACK MILES
(ix)	LEAFLETS.								
92	WELL.	8	8	-	19,000	15,000	17,000		
(x)	SPECIAL OPERATIONS.								
3		17		1					
100		5		-					
(xi)	FIGHTER PATROLS.								
100	MOS.	19	15	-					
(xii)	COLOGNE.								
8	MOS.	9	7	-	32,000	24,000	27,000	2,722	

3. ROUTE AND TIMING.

Route ordered to NURNBERG : 51.50N. 02.30E. - 50.30N. 04.35E. - 50.32N.
10.38E. - NURNBERG - 49.00N. 11.05E. - 48.30N. 09.20E. - 49.10N. 03.00E. 50.00N.
01.10E. - SELSEY BILL.

See route map attached.

Planned time of attack : 0110 - 0122 hrs.

Minelaying - ordered route : 54.30N. 05.00E. - 54.06N. 07.49E. (2305 -
2315 hrs) - Area - 54.30N. 05.00E.

4. WEATHER.

NURNBERG : 7/10 - 10/10 medium cloud in thin layers, occasionally breaking
to 5/10ths, tops 15,000 - 17,000 ft. Patches of cirrus, base 22,000 ft.
Visibility good through breaks. Wind at 21,000 ft. 275/60 degs.

Route to NURNBERG : Over English coast 7/10 - 8/10 convection cloud with
showers, tops 10 - 12,000 ft. Good clearances over south North Sea. Over Belgium
4/10 - 6/10ths st.-cu, tops 7 - 10,000 ft. Thence to about 20 miles north of
target small amounts only, then increasing to target. On return 6/10 - 8/10, tops
gradually lowering to 4 - 8,000 ft over N.E. France and breaking to small amounts
N. of Beauvais.

East of 07°E dense contrails persisted from 18 - 24,000 ft (P.F.F. report
contrails up to 30,000 ft over Ruhr).

Winds 21,000 ft. 280/35 degs, increasing to 275 - 280/60 degs towards
target area. On return 275/60 degs increasing to /70 degs to French Coast and
decreasing again over bases.

Bases : Fit for' take-off, but from 0400 - 0600 snow and sleet showers
spread over parts of Eastern England.

Minelaying areas : In the northern dropping areas there were occasional
heavy showers, with cloud top 16 - 20,000 ft and base 2,000 ft, lowering in showers
to 700 ft.

Moon : Half. Above horizon during operations.

5. E/A AND E/A ENCOUNTERED.

The majority of the very considerable number of enemy aircraft engaged or
encountered on this operation were part of the night fighter forces that maintained

/Page 3.....

Appendix E

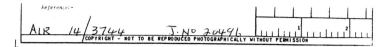
- 3 -

virtually a running battle with the bombers from midnight until 0130 hrs - a fight that lasted for nearly 250 miles in all, from the AACHEN area eastwards and then southwards to the target. On the long easterly leg, which was flown with a following wind, there were 50 combats and 77 sightings, of which 35 combats and 48 sightings involved twin engined enemy fighters. In the LIEGE-AACHEN area, where interceptions first occurred in any considerable number, the aircraft seen were nearly all single engined, but from the Rhine onwards JU.88's were reported in numbers far exceeding other types, of which ME.110's, ME.410's, ME.109's and FW.190's were seen or engaged in roughly equal numbers; a few DO.217's were seen but not involved in combat.

When the bombers turned southwards to their target both combats and sightings decreased, but over the target the following were reported :-

JU.88's	-	8 combats,	26	sightings.
ME.110's	-	2 "	8	"
ME.410's	-	1 "	5	"
U/i T/E	-	3 "	6	"
ME.109's	-	4 "	13	"
FW.190's	-	2 "	14	"
U/i S/E	-	1 "	9	"

After bombing, the number of combats was small - 3 T/E and 1 S/E on the short southerly leg, and on the return across Germany and N.E.France, 7 T/E and 3 S/E with very few sightings not involving combat.

7 enemy a/c are claimed destroyed by our forces before the attack on NURNBERG developed - a JU.88 by a 100 Group Mosquito in the BONN area, a ME.109 by a 4 Group Halifax south of BONN, a JU.88 and a ME.109 north of FRANKFURT by Lancasters of 5 Group, a FW.190 near FULDA by a 4 Group Halifax, and near BAMBERG a ME.110 by a 1 Group Lancaster.

In addition one JU.88 and one ME.210 are claimed as probably destroyed, and 5 JU.88's, 2 ME.110's and 2 ME.109's as damaged.

6. FLAK/SEARCHLIGHTS/OTHER AIDS TO DEFENCE.

Route : For reasons stated elsewhere in this report the bomber stream made its penetration into Germany on a much broader front than was intended and the general trend north of track gave the heavy defences in the AACHEN and COLOGNE-BONN areas much scope.

In this latter region large cones of searchlights, consisting of up to 80 beams, presented the guns with seen targets, and their fire was accurate, intense and effective. The defences of FRANKFURT were also in action and those aircraft that flew over SCHWEINFURT found the flak widespread, though inaccurate. On the return route STUTTGART sent up some intense fire and there was further trouble from STRASBOURG and LE TOUQUET, but other positions are, in view of the scatter, rather indeterminate.

Nurnberg : Heavy flak was fired in a moderate barrage with a ceiling of about 20,000 ft due to the presence of fighters. The increase in cloud as compared with the RHINE area made searchlights ineffective except as a means of silhouetting aircraft against the cloud and this proved very effective.

7. ENEMY FIGHTER REACTION.

Our bombers were plotted over England and south east to the SCHELDT estuary where already they were becoming dispersed. They crossed the coast at 2322 and eight minutes before that time fighters of NJG 1 and 4 were assembled from bases in Holland and Belgium and at 2325 hrs were diverted to the BONN area, though some reported making contact as far west as LIEGE. At 2332 hrs the force of minelayers

/Page 4......

Appendix E

- 4 -

having been correctly assessed, aircraft of NJG 3 were sent south to FRANKFURT, and this became the new area of general concentration. The fighters then followed the bombers to the target, which was announced at 0108 hrs - two minutes before zero hour - and a considerable number of fighters were present. Some of these apparently followed the withdrawing bombers on the way back to their own bases in France.

Victory claims were heard from one medium-range fighter in Holland, who reported two victims. NJG 5 was never heard and was presumably held in reserve against an attack on BERLIN.

8. ENEMY CLAIMS.

"The latest reports of the attack last night on the Reich territory show it to have been a unique catastrophe. The German air defences now report that at least 132 four-engined British bombers have been destroyed."

9. APPRECIATION.

The main target was NURNBERG and was approached from the N.N.W. after a long leg of 250 miles from NAMUR due east to the south of AACHEN and BONN and to the north of FRANKFURT and SCHWEINFURT. The only northerly diversion possible in the weather conditions of considerable convection cloud over the North Sea was a minelaying expedition of modest proportions. Small attacks by Pathfinder Mosquitoes were ordered on KASSEL, COLOGNE, AACHEN, DORTMUND, OBERHAUSEN and enemy airfields. It was unfortunate that cloud, which further north would have precluded the operation of a large force, failed altogether over part of the route between Belgium and the target, and left our aircraft exposed in the light of the half moon, with the added discomfiture of dense contrails once the Rhein was reached.

To this misfortune was added a change in wind, which proved less strong than expected and more westerly than north-westerly. At an early stage, therefore, our bombers were extended over a broad belt to the north of track, which took many over the towns of AACHEN, COLOGNE and BONN. The stream even extended as far south as the vicinity of FRANKFURT, though this was probably a result of the harassing by flak and fighters that by this time overtook the attackers. In these circumstances it is not surprising to find that some aircraft bombed SCHWEINFURT and other targets, some of them unidentified. On the homeward route this scatter became accentuated and aided individual fighters and defended areas to claim victims. The withdrawal from the Continent was to have been beyond the Samme, but in fact the bombers were spread over the whole area between the ordered track and the Belgian frontier.

The enemy at once discarded any idea of a serious threat from the north and concentrated his fighters, according to a simple plan, in the areas near BONN and FRANKFURT, from which the stream was readily intercepted. Once this had been achieved fighters were able to maintain contact in the moonlight. The target was named at 0113 hrs and the battle was resumed. Fighters returning westwards to their bases continued to attack.

The incidence of combats and sightings and of observations of aircraft shot down leaves little doubt that 59 aircraft were shot down by fighters between AACHEN and the final turning point. Thence to target three more were probably lost to the same cause, and over target five more were shot down by fighters. On the homeward route far more observations were made, apparently of a/c shot down by fighters, making a total loss in combat of 62 aircraft. There is strong evidence of a collision having occurred over the target. Flak seems to have caused the destruction of five bombers over target and further evidence can be adduced to account for losses to flak as follows : Namur 1; Aachen 1; Bonn 2; Koblenz 1; Schweinfurt 2; Strasbourg 1; Le Touquet 1 - a total of 14 a/c destroyed by ground defences.

Numerous other observations were made without cause of loss being visible and the total suggested is :

Fighters	- 62	(5 over target)
Collision	- 2	
Flak	- 14	
Unknown Causes	- 16	
	94	

H. A.B.C.
AIR STAFF INTELLIGENCE.
BC/S.27876/Int.
Issued at 18.00 hrs 12th April, 1944.

Appendix E

AIR 14/3744   J. N° 20496.

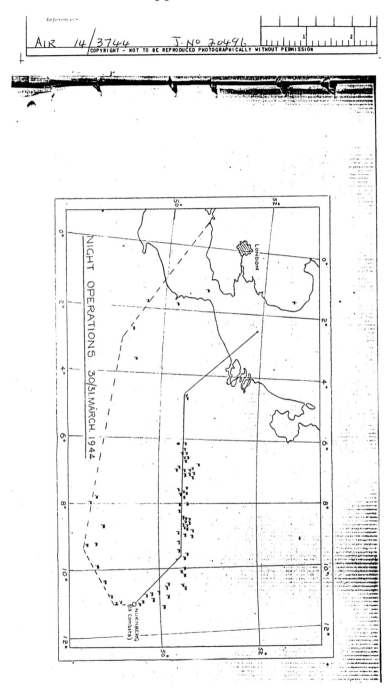

NIGHT OPERATIONS. 30/31.MARCH. 1944.

LONDON

NURNBERG
(23 Combats)

xxix

Appendix F

A.M.W.R.

EB 20 17 53

01510

958

SECRET.

INTERCEPTION/TACTICS NO. 35/45. NIGHT, 13th/14th FEBRUARY, 1945.

1. TARGETS & SORTIES.

TARGET	GROUP	TYPE OF A/C	SORTIES	ATTACKED TARGET	MISSING	HEIGHT 000 ft	TIME OVER TARGET
First Phase.							
i) BOHLEN	4,6,3		368	324	1 (.3%)	14-24½	2154-2212
(S. of Leipzig)	4	HAL.	211	198	1	15-19	2154-2212
	6	HAL.	115	108	-	14-20	2157-2211
	8	LANC.	34	21	-	14-18	2154-2206
		MOS.	8	7	-	18-24½	2156-2202
ii) DRESDEN	5		254	244	1 (.4%)	1-16	2203-2228
(1st attack)		LANC	245	235	1	10-16	2203-2228
		MOS.	9	9	-	800-3	2205-2208
iii) MAGDEBURG	8	MOS.	62	61	-	11-26	2130-2141
(1st attack)							
iv) NURNBERG	8	MOS.	3	7	-	33	2159-2215
v) DORTMUND	8	MOS.	6	5	-	28-33	2101-2106
Second Phase.							
vi) DRESDEN	1,3,6,8		551	524	4 (.7%)	7-21	0121-0155
(2nd attack)	1	LANC	261	248	2	14-20	0123-0152
	3	LANC	162	151	1	15-21	0125-0155
	6	LANC	67	65	-	17-19	0127-0145
	8	LANC	61	60	1	7-19	0121-0145
vii) BONN (Point)	8	MOS.	16	16	-	18-22	0014-0024
viii) MAGDEBURG	8	MOS.	9	9	-	25-28	0056-0112
(2nd attack)							
ix) MISBURG	8	MOS.	9	7	-	27-30	0130-0147
(Nr. Hanover)							
Other Activity.							
x) BOMBER SUPPORT	100	M,H,S,Lib,F	117	107	-		
xi) SIGNALS PATROLS	100	M,H.	7	5	-		
xii) MET. RECCE.	8	MOS.	1	1	-		
TOTAL			1,407	1,310	6 (.4%)		

2. ROUTES AND TIMING ORDERED.

Bohlen : Reading - 5000N 0200E - 5000N 0600E - 5055N 0850E - Bohlen - 5100N 1240E - 5030N 1155E - 5045N 1035E - 5029N 0900E - 5040N 0755E - 5010N 0530E - 5015N 0350E - Orfordness.
T.O.T. 2153-2209 hrs.   Over Continent 1945-0100 hrs.

Dresden : Reading - 5000N 0200E - 5000N 0500E - 5100N 0600E - 5110N 0800E - 5143N
(1st) 1020E - 5135N 1240E - Dresden - 5055N 1355E - 5025N 1355E - 5020N 1310E - 4915N 1150E - 4825N 0900E - 4830N 0710E - 4900N 0500E - Orfordness.
T.O.T. 2206-2208 hrs.   Over Continent 1953-0240 hrs.

Dresden : Reading - 5000N 0200E - 4945N 0905E - 4955N 1030E - 5050N 1200E - Dresden -
(2nd) 5055N 1355E - 5030N 1240E - 4915N 1150E - 4830N 0920E - 4830N 0710E - 4900N 0500E - Orfordness.
T.O.T. 0124-0145 hrs.   Over Continent 2258-0535 hrs.

See route map for routes to Magdeburg, Bonn, Nurnberg, Misberg and the above targets.

/Page 2.....

XXX

Appendix F

- 2 -

3. BOMBER SUPPORT AND SECURITY.

    Bohlen and Dresden (1st) : Mandrel Screen - 10 Hals, 2005-2117hrs, 5038N 0540E - 4)44N 0543E, moving at 2110 hrs to 5132N 0530E - 5038N 0540E, jamming 2150-2300 hrs. Window - 8 Hals, 2 Libs, made a feint against Mainz-Mannheim area, 2043-2144hrs, mean positions 5000N 0600E - to points from 4958N 0810E to 4)25N 0759E, thence to 4)25N 0748E. Intruders - See below.

    Dresden (2nd) : Mandrel Screen, 2 Hals, 8 Stir, positions as for 1st screen, jamming 2350-0030 hrs and 0100-0230 hrs. Window - 9 Libs and 1 Hal made a feint against Koln-Koblenz area, 0001-0035 hrs, mean positions 4952N 0550E - 5024N 0633E, jamming out to 5050N 0650E, 5040N 0656E and 5027N 0705E, thence to 5010N 0500E. ABC Lancs were in the main force.

    Intruders : High level - 56 Mos; claimed 2 Mo.110's destroyed N of Frankfurt; 19 other chases unsuccessful owing to interference. Low level - 3 Mos. Fighter Command intruders - 21 Mos high level and 3 Mos low level.

    Jostle & Piperack : 7 Forts and 1 Mos completed.
    Security : Radar and Signals silence to 0600E.

4. WEATHER.

Moon	: Nil.
Bohlen & Dresden (1st)	: 9-10/10ths Sc, tops 9,000ft, some medium cloud at 15,000ft. Wind at 18,000ft, 260 degs, 70 mph. Route: From the French coast 10/10ths cloud rising to 15,000ft in frontal belt 0200-0400E, lowering onstward. Icing in frontal belt. Return similar with little cloud west of 0500E.
Dresden (2nd)	: 3-7/10ths variable drifting cloud patches, top 6,000ft. Wind at 20,000ft, 265 degs, 85 mph. Route: Clear to 0400E, then frontal belt with cloud to 17,000ft with rime and static, breaking east of 0900E to 3-6/10ths, tops 6,000ft.
Other targets	: Magdeburg (1st) 9-10/10ths, tops 10-12,000ft; (2nd) 10/10ths Ci, tops 26,000ft. Bonn: 10/10ths A/S, tops 12,15,000ft. Dortmund: 9-10/10ths Sc, tops 10-12,000ft, and an A/S layer top 22,000ft. Nurnberg : 3-6/10ths, top 10-15,000ft. Hanover : 10/10ths, tops 10,000ft.
Enemy A/Fs	: Mainly fit, but rain and thick cloud in frontal belt.

5. ENEMY FIGHTER REACTION.

    Bohlen and Window feint : 2022-2046, 3 JD control active. 2022, 3 JD plotted a/c SW of Vogelsang and W of Koblenz flying east. 2031, 3 JD plotted a/c NE of Lisbun, flying east. 2045, II NJG 6 (?) sent to a position between Karlsruhe and Heilbronn. 2053, II NJG 6 to beacon Dachs (N of Mannheim). 2055, IV NJG 6 to beacon Otto (near Hanau). 2102, II NJG 6 to Dachs at top speed. 2105, IV NJG 6 to a point 10 miles W of Mainz. 2108, Large formations plotted over a broad front W of a line Koblenz-Bingen. 2108-2213, Bohlen force plotted to the target area. 2115, II NJG 6 told the main force was probably flying east along the latitude of Frankfurt. Further plots on the Window feint. 2124-9, NJG 6 a/c to fly to Otto. 2135, IV NJG 6 sent to the Kassel area but did not do so and at 2137 were told to land at Kilzingen, as were II NJG 6 at Schwabisch Hall. Two recce a/c of II NJG 6 stayed up near Nurnberg till 0245 hrs.

    2204, Plotting on the Bohlen raid between Jena and NE Leipzig. 2213-29, Plots on the homeward route and a route WNW to Kassel area.

    Dresden (1st) : 2026-28, 3 JD gave plots in the Cologne area on a/c flying NE. 2102-2213, Plots as far as N of Leipzig, followed by a gap till 2232, when bombers were reported leaving the target. 2233-2310, 1 JD plotted the return past Chemnitz to near Nurnberg. 2315-0025, Heavy plotting from E of Nurnberg to Strasbourg.

    Dresden (2nd) :0022-0057, Jafue Middle Rhein gave plots W of Koblenz on a/c flying east. 0025, Plot on 8 four-engined a/c 40 miles W of Mainz. 0025-0337, Plotting on the Dresden route, assessed at 0052 as 300 a/c. 0110-0120, Probably

/Page 3......

Appendix F

- 3 -

I NJG 6 made a second sortie, and were given plots S of Weimar. 0111, I NJG 6 told the main attack was on Magdeburg. 0123, All reported a/c flying towards Dresden. 0148, NJG 10 given the target. 0149-0220, Jafue Middle Rhein gave plots between Chemnitz and Schweinfurt. 0205-16, NJG 10 to land at Finow.

6. ATTACKS AND COMBATS.

Bohlen : Outward ed at target there were no combats. Homeward: Leaving Bohlen 2300hrs, a attack by an U/I a/c and 1 combat with S/E E/A. East of Bonn, 2359hrs, 1 T/E E/A attacked, and over Belgium, 0035hrs, one U/I E/A was fired on.

Dresden (1st) : Outward: E of Dusseldorf, 2103 and 2110 hrs, 2 combats. S of Magdeburg, 2145 and 2150, one attack by T/E E/A and 1 combat with a suspected jet a/c. 8 a/c reported seeing 4 jet a/c between 1000E and the target, but none attacked. A few T/E E/A were seen near Leipzig,and at target, 2209-2219hrs, 10 S/E and T/E were reported, but there was no fire. Homeward: No incidents.

Dresden (2nd) : Outward: Approaching and crossing the Rhine 0033-0059hrs, 3 attacks and 1 combat. S of Schweinfurt, 0103 hrs, 1 attack, and on the next leg there was 1 combat with a JU.88 at 0112 hrs. Target area: 0134 hrs, 1 combat with S/E E/A, and 0142 hrs 1 T/E attacked. Homeward: S.E. of Nurnberg, 0236 and 0254hrs, 2 JU.88's attacked. S of Stuttgart, 0313hrs, 1 combat with JU.88, and W of Strasbourg, 0413hrs, 1 combat with T/E E/A.

7. GROUND DEFENCES.

Bohlen (9-10/10ths) : A few S/Ls attempted to find cloud gaps. H.F. was moderate at first, mainly predictor control unseen, and decreased during the attack. Some guns from Zeitz were in action. Few a/c were damaged. Route : H.F. slight from Koblenz and Fulda.

Dresden (1st) (9-10/10ths) : Markers at 800-3,500ft met no flak. No S/Ls; H.F. negligible. 3 A/c only were damaged. Route : H.F. slight from Cologne when crossing the Rhine, and H.F. negligible N of Bitterfeld.

Dresden (2nd) (3-7/10ths) : No S/Ls. H.F. negligible, barrage mainly below the average bombing height. Route: Little opposition but a few a/c were engaged at Darmstadt, Chemnitz, Zeitz, Brux and Augsburg.

8. APPRECIATION.

Deep penetrations by overland route into Central Germany had been in abeyance for almost a month when the occasion arose for a heavy attack on Dresden, which had become vitally important to Germany's Eastern Front. During that interval the enemy had transferred some of his night fighters to the East - presumably for ground attack work against the Russians - but otherwise the situation was unchanged from what it was in January, when deep incursions were made to Leuna, Magdeburg, Zeitz and Brux with very moderate losses.

The presence of a frontal belt north to south across the Continent, with a good deal of cloud to the east of it, played a large part in the operational plan. It was decided that 5 Group Lancasters should attack Dresden at 2215hrs and 4 and 6 Group Halifaxes should take a high priority oil target at Bohlen, just S of Leipzig at 2200hrs. After a lapse of over 3 hrs, at 0130 hrs, Lancasters of 1, 3 and 6 Groups should make a second attack on Dresden.

In the first phase cloud cover was to be utilised to an unusual degree. In view of the inability of searchlights to operate below cloud and the enemy's known reluctance to waste ammunition on unseen aircraft, it was decided to send 5 Group between Dusseldorf and Cologne, with all the advantages that concealed approach over the battle area could bring, and hence they were to fly N of Kassel and Leipzig to

/Page 4.....

Appendix F

Reference:-

AIR 14/3745   T. No 20496

- 4 -

Dresden, crossing the defended area at Bitterfeld, N of Leipzig. 4 and 6 Groups were to cross the Rhine just north of Koblenz and keep south of Kassel and Leipzig, taking the more direct route both out and home that their endurance dictated, while 5 Group were further to extend the enemy's defences by returning south of Nurnberg, Stuttgart and Strasbourg. In this phase it was expected that the approach of the Bohlen raid over SW Germany would be much more free from cloud than the north, and there lay the danger from the German night fighters. It was accordingly arranged that No.100 Group should put up a convincing feint by means of Window, spreading out eastwards from N Luxembourg to cover the whole area from Mainz to Mannheim and so attract 7 JD's fighters, while the Halifaxes slipped through on the other side of Koblenz. Mosquitoes of 8 Group were also to make feint attacks in the south on Nurnberg and in the north on Magdeburg.

In the later phase the front would have moved further east, and the plan for this stage of the night's work was to feint with Window northwards from Luxembourg to the Rhine to a line from Cologne to Koblenz, and to send the Lancasters, not through the "Frankfurt gap", but across the Mainz-Mannheim defended belt, relying on cloud to defeat the searchlights and flak, and on the exhaustion of the fighter effort after a period of about 3 hours' activity against the first phase.

These plans proved entirely successful in protecting the approach of all the forces used. Further, the enemy's mistakes in reading Bomber Command's intentions and in the resultant deployment of his fighters ended in an abject failure of his whole defence system. Only 6 bombers were lost, of a total of 1400 despatched.

The formidable fighter forces in 2 JD (NW Germany) were presumably grounded in common with those of 3 JD North of Frankfurt, for they were never heard. The fighters of all three Gruppen of 7 JD (SW Germany) and one of Jafue Middle Rhine (Frankfurt) were directed to oppose what was adjudged to be the main force and covered the west of the Mainz-Mannheim area against the Window feint until 2115hrs, when the whole of the main forces were well across the Rhine farther north. NJG 6 sent up recce a/c to attempt to clarify the situation, but the control evidently regarded the position as hopeless. Two Gruppen landed, one probably attempted to pursue, and II NJG 2 (Mainz) apparently waited near Limburg for return.

Meanwhile 1 JD plotted both the Dresden and the Bohlen forces in to their targets, though, bearing in mind the lack of fighters based inland in this JD, it is thought few a/c were controlled. Those that were up may well have been misled by the fact that the force was plotted returning WNW from Bohlen towards Kassel - a direction taken only by the few early Windowing Mosquitoes of 8 Group while the main force flew a dog-leg track WSW back to Koblenz where it is possible that II NJG 2 attempted to intercept. The Dresden force was not plotted between 2213hrs, when leaving target, and 2228 hrs. The south-about return was then closely followed, without producing any combats.

The policy of crossing the cloud-covered defences in the Rhine/was area completely justified in the first phase, and in the second the similar crossing of the Middle Rhine near Darmstadt caused no trouble. There were a few fighters up in this area, and 4 of them attacked our a/c between 0730 and 1030E, but the numbers cannot have been large and contact was not maintained. Indeed, the Window feint was again assessed as the main force till the bombers were 100 miles east of the battle line. At the target only a few fighters were present, there being only one attack. These were probably from the Berlin area, as they were ordered to land at Finow at 0202 hrs. South of Nurnberg there was a little more activity.

Nowhere was flak troublesome on this night - neither in the defended areas crossed on route nor at the targets and not one crew reports a single loss to this cause. On the other hand the losses on the second Dresden raid are not fully unexplained. The observations included a collision between a bomber and a T/E fighter SE of Frankfurt, an a/c falling into the sea when approaching the Somme Estuary, at least one loss at the target and one E of Stuttgart, possibly through a fighter.

/Page 5.....

Appendix F

- 5 -

The losses are ascribed as follows :-

	Flak	Fighters	Collision	Bombs	Unknown
Bohlen	-	-	-	-	1
Dresden (1st)	-	-	-	1	-
Dresden (2nd)	-	1	1	-	2
TOTAL	-	1	1	1	3

H.Q.B.C.
AIR STAFF INTELLIGENCE.
BC/S.278/6/Int.).
Issued at 1800hrs 18th February 1945.

Appendix F

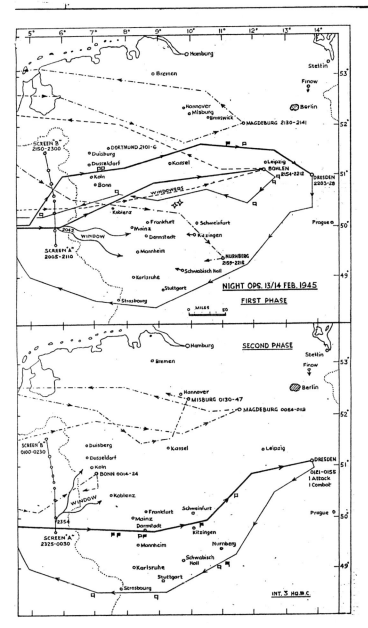

NIGHT OPS. 13/14 FEB. 1945

FIRST PHASE

SECOND PHASE

INT. 3 HQ.B.C.